The Sensible Stage: Staging and the Moving Image

A collection of newly commissioned texts that explore the moving image in relation to performance, time and the event.*

Edited by

BRIDGET CRONE

Published by Picture This with Plenty Projects
First published 2012

ISBN 978-0-9554961-2-7
A catalogue record for this book is available from the British Library.

Editor (and concept): Bridget Crone
Designed by Modern Activity
Printed and bound by Lecturis in the Netherlands

Picture This
40 Sydney Row, Bristol, BS1 6UU
office@picture-this.org.uk
picture-this.org.uk

Bridget Crone / Plenty Projects
info@plentyprojects.org
plentyprojects.org

Distributed to the book trade by Cornerhouse
cornerhouse.org

Thanks to all of the contributors and artists especially those that provided images: Clare Gasson, Annabel Nicolson, Carolee Schneeman, Beatrice Gibson, Anja Kirschner and David Panos, Jimmy Robert, Yael Davids, Cara Tolmie, Gail Pickering, Marc Chaimowicz, Charlotte Moth, Marcelline Delbecq.

Thanks also to: Polly Braden, Benjamin Cook, Therese Keogh, Dan Kidner, Elie During, Marie-Anne McQuay, Sam Nightingale, Simon O'Sullivan, Lisa Panting, Clara Plasencia, Jane Porter, Alexandra Roche, Lucy A Sames

Monash University, Melbourne generously supported the development of this book through their Visiting Artists Scheme.

* Alain Badiou & Elie During's conversation is translated from French by Oliver Feltham. Reprinted with permission from: *A Theater without Theater*, exhib. cat. (Barcelona and Lisbon: MACBA / Fundaçao de Arte Moderna e Contemporanea and Colecçao Berardo, Lisboa, 2007)

lecturis
printing company

The Henry Moore Foundation

ARTS COUNCIL ENGLAND

LOTTERY FUNDED

CONTENTS

The essays that make up *The Sensible Stage: Staging and the Moving Image* have been newly commissioned, with the exception of the re-published conversation between Alain Badiou and Elie During. The programmes of Picture This and Media Art Bath over the last five years provide the prism through which this collection is focused. Continuity is provided by the inclusion of Lisa Panting's essay on Yael Davids – Lisa was director of Picture This from 2009 to 2011, and commissioned the performance work *Learning to Imitate in Absentia* (2011). The book also connects with the future programme at Picture This through the inclusion of new writing on the work of Jimmy Robert and Cara Tolmie, both of whom have been commissioned by the organisation to make new work in 2012.

I'd like to thank Bridget Crone for her tireless work on the book, and for bringing together such a fantastic line-up of contributors willing to collaborate and discuss their ideas during the process of putting the book together. I'd also like to thank Modern Activity for their great work on the design of the book, and Arts Council England and The Henry Moore Foundation who supported the project.

Dan Kidner
Director, Picture This

The Sensible Stage: Staging and the Moving Image

BRIDGET CRONE

The arena, the card-table, the magic circle, the temple, the stage, the screen, the tennis court, the court of justice, etc., all are in form and function play-grounds, i.e. forbidden spots, isolated, hedged around, hallowed, within which special rules obtain.

__ Johan Huizinga quoted in Eugene Thacker, *In the Dust of This Planet* (1)

The essays in *The Sensible Stage: Staging and the Moving Image* seek to occupy that creative terrain where practice and ideas meet, an exercise in bringing theory and practice together. Unfolding around the concept of 'staging', *The Sensible Stage: Staging and the Moving Image* invokes the boundaries of presence and participation inherent in performance practices by addressing the work of artists whose practice involves both moving image and performance in a way that questions the definition of these terms. These are continuing debates and speculations on topics that range from the prevalence of artwork exploring a textual dimension, to the intense questioning of the status and presence of the image, and to the use of theatricality and theatrical procedures. What follows, therefore, is a *rapprochement* between thought and practice, or rather, practice and the practice of thought.

The Sensible Stage: Staging and the Moving Image addresses the work of contemporary artists whose practices question conventional definitions of performance and moving image culture. Therefore, rather than simply understood as the relationship between active and passive bodies, as much contemporary art as well as theatre and performance practice is conventionally considered, the artists discussed here invoke questions of materiality, of appearance, and of affect in their practices: questions that invigorate a discussion of these assumed oppositions within image culture. In this way, the use of the term 'staging' provides us with a means to articulate the way in which images and bodies appear temporally and spatially in the present moment. And most importantly, 'staging' is a way of both complicating and re-imagining the division between body and image; between what is experienced and what is imagined, what is immediate and what is mediated, and what is live and what is not-live. Yet, as we know, performance and moving image practices in the last fifty years have already radically disrupted these neat separations between the live-ness of the body and the not-live state of the image: the film-performances of Carolee Schneemann, for example, the body and the film-image combine in the moment of the performance to produce and affect one another (Schneemann's work is discussed in this book in an essay by Lucy Reynolds). Within this context, staging becomes a means for re-thinking and re-configuring the relationship between body and image, between immediate experience and mediated information, between projected image and performed body, and between the stage and the screen.

fig. 2 — *The Sensible Stage* began as a performance programme in 2007, designed to explore questions of participation and theatricality in relation to performance.(2) Plotting a path that responded to Jacques Rancière's essay, 'The Emancipated Spectator' and the pervasive influence of Nicolas Bourriaud's *Relational Aesthetics*, the programme sought to question the way that 'participation' had entered the lexicon of contemporary art practices without seriously excavating the notions of bodily presence, liveness and appearance to which it was subscribed. Furthermore, it seemed that there was a concurrent and burgeoning interest in performance in contemporary art, an interest that was marked by the use of re-enactment and forms of theatre. Unlike those working in the well-established field of Live Art, these contemporary artists seemed interested in articulating a sense of separation, whether that is an articulation between the 'live' unfolding performance and the quoted or re-enacted material; or, a separation between audience and performer-artist in a manner contrary to the well-established *raison d'être* of performance art 'happening anywhere anytime'; or finally, the bounded-nature of the performance as a temporal event with a distinct beginning and ending point. Practitioners who explore these productive disjunctures include London-based artists, Pil and Galia Kollectiv, Clare Gasson, Yael Davids and Gail Pickering whose work is included in this book as well as the Australian artist, Tom Nicholson, whose collaboration with composer Andrew Byrne, *Lines Towards Another Century* (2008) combined the unbounded ethereal qualities of sound and the projected image with the particular temporal and structural properties of a list, an instructional score and a live performance.(3) Similarly, Yael Davids' *Learning to Imitate in Absentia* (2011), commissioned and produced by Picture This and discussed here in an essay by Lisa Panting, sought to address the way in which the space between bodies and between the body, object and voice structure the 'stage' of the performance within the space of the gallery.

The inter-relationship between the body and the image – the moving image, the projected image, the imagined image – is a strong thread running through *The Sensible Stage: Staging and the Moving Image*. As Lucy Reynolds points out in her essay, 'The Subject in Process', expanded cinema practices of the 1960s and 70s established a relationship between the body and the image as live process unfolding through and by performance. The unfurling of the hidden mechanics or apparatus of film, and its subsequent 'live' manipulation or play, such as in the work of Malcolm Le Grice, created an immersive situation in which artist, audience and image were joined in the mutuality of the unfolding experience. However, this experience of the image as one in which we are constantly swept up has been re-invigorated and re-examined by many of the artists' practices discussed in this book. Therefore, as important as it is to note that the dichotomy between the live presence of the body and the mediated presence of the image has been broken down by expanded cinema practices, it is crucial to observe the way in which these distinctions are being re-configured in more recent practices that involve the moving image and performance. This is to say that the body's role in generating or producing the image is disrupted by a splitting of the productive relationship of body and image into new questions – questions that consider the materiality of film, the projection of the body as image, the separation of voice from the body, and the use of structuring devices to puncture, divide and manipulate the smooth articulation of time in the present moment.

Following on from *The Sensible Stage* performance programme, a further programme of performances and discussion attempted to address the manner in which text and body come together to produce the stage of experience, of the performance, of the event. *A Theatre to Address: a festival of textual form / concrete /*
fig. 1 *material / scripted / performed* (2010) specifically sought to understand the relation of text (as an abstract structuring device) to the body; where text might be a force that conditions the appearance or languages of the body and the body itself, a force for the appearance of language as is the case in Beatrice Gibson's performance-lecture, *A scripted talk on the script and the score* (2010), which features in this book.(4) In this way, *A Theatre to Address* responded to the French philosopher, Alain Badiou's equation *body and text meeting in the presence of live bodies produces theatre* through examining each of these entities: body, text, performance, in relation to the production and appearance of images, whether projected, imagined or 'to be imagined'.

A central concern, therefore, was the possibility of staging as an event that punctured the smooth space of experience exploring a range of methods from the estrangement of Bertolt Brecht's epic theatre to the bodily action inherent in Vsevolod Meyerhold's theatre of gesture. Cara Tolmie's work takes up the muteness of the voice in relation to the experience of the body; as Isla Leaver-Yap suggests in her essay, 'The Gesture of the Muted Voice': '[T]he mute voice might not say anything but it can still sound, still gesture. What, then, is the gesture of the muted voice?'.[5] Here the body is a force that drives the external expression of gesture, voice or image.

The manner in which the stage is made visible by the obvious structuring device of text, script and the collection and editing of images, and the very existence of the structures of the stage makes apparent the architectonics of power inherent in our world. These strategies lead us back in a circular fashion to questions of what, when and where is the stage? What is live and what is mediated? What is experienced and what is imagined? Badiou, for example, whose conversation with Elie During opens *The Sensible Stage: Staging and the Moving Image*, provides a clear approach to these questions, stating that cinema is always consigned to the past. It is always a recorded and therefore deferred moment: 'cut from the present', it is a 'visitation' from the past, he suggests.[6] Theatre, on the other hand, is always live for Badiou: it is an event that is produced through the meeting of text and body in the presence of an audience. The contingent nature of the body means that the event of the performance can never be repeated but is always realised anew. And the fact that this meeting takes place in the presence of an audience, itself a collection of bodies, a potential 'public', ensures the singularity and instability of its form.

The stage or space of performance is produced through the establishing of a set of rules or instructions but it is not wholly reduced to this. As Badiou suggests in 'A Theatre of Operations' (reproduced here), there is a whole set of contingencies or chance-events at work in the expression of what he terms, the theatre-idea; these are connected to the aleatory nature of the body. He states: '[t]heater is a complex ordering system whose material series is not set in stone: texts of course, but also bodies, costumes, the set, the site, music, light...'[7] There are several points in Badiou and During's conversation that are important for us to take up in our discussion of staging and the moving image: these are primarily concerned with the manner in which the space of the stage is organised in relation to what Badiou terms, 'theatre', and the relation of time and the moving image to this space of the theatre. Badiou differentiates theatre from the 'plastic arts' through the manner in which it organises time: theatre is the product of the organisation and display of bodies in such a way as to demonstrate the 'evident primacy of time over space' whereas plasticity is produced through the display of the primacy of space over time. There is a distinction therefore between different organisations of *time* so that video for example displayed in a temporal manner might be considered as theatre whereas video displayed on a monitor exhibits a plasticity that results from the abandonment of the movement of time in favour of an emphasis on the spatial dimensions of exhibition. This, of course, equates with our understanding of cinema *as performance,* an understanding developed through expanded cinema practices in which the performed-cinematic image becomes visible to us through the assemblage of bodies and structures in the singular event of the performance. This brings us to the second important point that arises in Badiou and During's conversation, and this is that for Badiou theatre is the product of the body-language dialectic: it is produced through the coming together of 'the body and a text' in the present moment in the space of the stage. The image, therefore, is considered only a dimension of the body or language, and cinema itself is always, cut from the present, signaling a withdrawal from the visible into the past.

Those of us familiar with a form of cinema that is performed 'live' through the inter-relationship of body and image, the distinction between the singular, live event of theatre and the inherent remove and repetition of cinema is difficult to accept. Instead, we understand that the performance of cinema itself is akin to the singular and live nature of theatre as is demonstrated by many of the works discussed in this book. This is the suggestion that both theatre and cinema can be 'live' and that they produce new ideas through the event of their performance. As Badiou suggests: 'The [theatre-] idea arises in and by the performance, through the act of theatrical representation. The idea is irreducibly theatrical and does not pre-exist before its arrival "on stage".' (8) If we consider a particular form of *performed*-cinema in this way, we might consider the image to be at times like a body and at times operating in the manner of a text. This is not to suggest that the image in this case is a dimension of the body or of language but that it operates as body, or as language or text: the image interacts with the body, for example, within the event of the performance so that rather than being an announcement from the past (the arrival of pre-existing information), it too is produced through the performance. For example, Jimmy Robert's work confounds the separation that Badiou suggests between the time of performance and the plasticity of exhibition. His work, *L'Education Sentimentale* (2005) and the more recent, *consensus rouge noir (Bristol)* (2012) commissioned and produced by Picture This, layers images and scripts from past works (Robert's own, and in the case of *L'Education Sentimentale,* the work of Bas Jan Ader) into a present performance: a performance that is so open ended as to demand the response and interaction of the audience in producing these images anew. Therefore, in these works, the image exists in a transitory state on a smooth continuum from past to future tense. In being cut from the past, the images in the *consensus rouge noir* series of works are performed in the present and realised through this performance so that the separation between the present state of the body and the past-remove of the cinematic image is confused.

This question of the 'live' / not-live-ness of the cinematic image and performance is discussed by Ian White in his essay, 'Performer, Audience, Mirror: Cinema, Theatre and the Idea of the Live', which was based on seminar series that he gave in London over the last two years: *6 or more kinds of theatre*, held at no.w.here (2010), and *Performer, Audience, Mirror: Cinema, Theatre and the Idea of the Live*, LUX (2011). White seeks to radically negate notions of live-ness attached to both performance and cinema in order to be able to re-consider them both as equally not-live and live. In undertaking this exercise, White turns his focus to the architecture of the theatre in order to examine the way in which ideas of participation (and non-participation) have evolved through the notion of the agora as the site of democratic participation. Citing, Dorothy Richardson's article from 1928, '[T]he new film can assist radio in turning the world into a vast council chamber', White asks us to consider both cinema and performance as unstable entities that act to enclose and to separate the viewer from a participation in the frame.[9] This instability of the feedback loop – of performance into image, image into performance and so on – also acts to undermine fixities of time, reminding us of the relation nature of time itself.

White's act of negating, simultaneously, both sides of the live / mediation dialectic acts to open up a new terrain of possibility, mirrored in Pil and Galia Kollectiv's essay, 'The Divided Stage: Splitting the Dialectics of Performance'. Here Pil and Galia Kollectiv evoke Badiou's concept of 'splitting', in order to question the ethical formulations of allegiance and agency in relation to the performance, 'Be Black, Baby!', which takes place within Brian De Palma's film *Hi, Mom!* (1973). Splitting is the term given to the act of re-making (or as Badiou says, 'forcing') a separation between things that are assumed to be one, so that, in terms of the operations of theatre, this provides us with new ways of re-configuring the division between image and body, stage and screen: that is, between what is considered live and what is mediated.(10) While Pil and Galia Kollectiv's essay is primarily concerned with the ethical nature of theatre practice, the discussion of *a performance of* a performance (the enactment of cultural and racial stereotypes) within a film further complicates conceptions of time within our discussion of the live / not-live nature of performance, theatre and the image. William Rubin, the main protagonist in De Palma's film, is engaged in the act of surreptitiously filming his neighbours. This act of *imaging* those around him is a process that becomes enveloped in his daily life and results in his involvement with the black activist theatre group that stages, 'Be Black, Baby!', and therefore, Rubin's immersion and emergence into the image at once evokes the complexities of image culture today. Unlike, the act of voyeurism in Alfred Hitchcock's *Rear Window* (1954), in which the protagonist is separated from and looks through the window to the image outside (and outside of himself), Rubin's voyeurism is without this frame: instead, Rubin enters into the image both producing, experiencing and acting within the images he produces.(11) However, while Rubin enters into the image by participating in his neighbours' theatre performance, for example, the staging of the performance within the film provides a direct contrast to the boundless nature of the imagining technology of Rubin's voyeurism: it produces a live moment within a mediated image.

The 'live' performance of 'Be Black, Baby' is both a mediated image (transmitted, as it is, through the medium of film) and experienced by us as 'live'. As Pil and Galia Kollectiv point out this results in a confusion of reaction: our judgement and disgust at the reactions of the (not-live) audience in the film and at the same time, the immediacy of our own reactions as an audience means that our allegiances are challenged. In this case, the 'remove' of the cinematic image is denied twice: once by the boundless and time-less nature of the technology of Rubin's imaging (or imagination), and secondly by the performance of *the performance* of the image, that is the performance of stereotypes captured and re-performed, experienced and re-experienced as mediated *and* live. The London-based artist, fig. 3 __ Gail Pickering's work, *Brutalist Premolition* (2008) exercised something similar in its realisation as a live performance and film projection within a sculptural set.(12) Here too, the boundary between live action and projected images is a complexity of unexpected splits and layers. Taking place in an abstract-replica of an existing architectural form (one of the flats in the infamous Robin Hood Gardens Estate in Poplar, East London), the 'live' performance of actors on stage directly replicated their performance in the film also projected onto the stage. The mirroring of mediated and live-action in the mirrored spaces of the stage-set and the apartment acted to emphasise the reception and transmission of images within the performance itself. In this case, the use of actors recognisable from TV soap operas set them at a remove and flattened their live presence into images mediated by the screen. Pickering's work typically confronts conventions of live-ness and transmission so that in her desire to approach the singular intensity of the body in performance, she unravels the constitution of the live presence of the body through a complex array of transmitted images: images transmitted technologically or through cultural stereotype, she layers the two together.

The Sensible Stage: Staging and the Moving Image proposes staging as a method for the (re) articulation of the myriad ways in which the relationship between body and image is realised through moving image and performance practice today. As a result of its intimate relationship with theatre (from where the term originates), staging is an inherently divisive device pitting audience against actor, action against spectatorship, live experience against mediated image. Yet, at the same time, staging is a methodology that allows us to re-examine these divisions and to remake the ways in which the image and body are mutually bound together. This is signalled in general terms through a movement away from methodologies that act to dissolve the temporal and spatial boundaries between performer, audience and what is performed in favour of a reinstatement of the spaces of the stage and the screen. To put it in another way, this is a movement away from performance art ('Live Art') to theatre. Furthermore, the attention paid to structuring devices, in many of the practices discussed in this book, acts as a means to address and understand the expanded economies through which both images and bodies move.

This is the awareness that we participate in an economy that operates through the boundlessness of the sensory effects of images. Therefore, while 'staging' offers a method for practice in terms of enabling new combinations and configurations of the tension between image and body (the act of 'splitting' that Pil and Galia Kollectiv discuss in their essay), it also provides a bounded space – a space in which 'special rules' govern the appearance of things (perhaps bodies, perhaps images) within its bounds. In contrast to the unbridled nature of sensory effects, we have a stage; it's a space defined for action, discourse and discussion: '[T]he arena, the card-table, the magic circle, the temple, the stage, the screen... forbidden spots, isolated, hedged around, hallowed, within which special rules obtain.'(13)

ENDNOTES

(1) Johan Huizinga, *Homo Ludens: A Study of the Play Element in Culture* (Boston: Beacon Books, 1971), p. 10. Quoted in Eugene Thacker, *In the Dust of This Planet* (Alesford, UK: Zero Books, 2011), p. 56.

(2) *The Sensible Stage* (2007): Lucienne Cole, Melanie Gilligan, Pil and Galia Kollectiv. Cube Microplex, Bristol; Holburne Museum, Bath; and Widcombe Social Club, Widcombe.
The Sensible Stage was further conceptualised as a screening programme as part of *LUX's New Work* (2008) programme, and which included work by: Lucienne Cole, Pil and Galia Kollectiv, Mikko Canini, Louisa Fairclough and Gail Pickering.

(3) Andrew Byrne and Tom Nicholson, *Lines Towards Another Century* (2008): audio-visual installation (surround sound, video projection and monitors), score for string quartet and actor performed by the Elysian Quartet, list of all of the national boundaries created during the 20th century. Commissioned by Media Art Bath, 2008.

(4) *A Theatre to Address: a festival of textual form / concrete / material / scripted / performed* (2010) Clare Gasson, Maryam Jafri, Pil and Galia Kollectiv, Sovay Berriman (with Luis Alvarez, Paul Cordwell, Joe Devlin and Magnus Quaife), Phil Coy, Annabel Frearson, Beatrice Gibson, Julika Gittner, The Otolith Group, Arnolfini, Bristol.

(5) Isla Leaver-Yap, 'The Gesture of the Muted Voice: Cara Tolmie's *Myriad Mouth Line*', in *The Sensible Stage: Staging and the Moving Image*, ed. Bridget Crone (Bristol: Picture This, 2012), pp. 145-151.

(6) Alain Badiou, 'The False Movements of Cinema', in *Handbook of Inaesthetics*, trans. Alberto Toscano (Stanford: Stanford University Press, 2005), p. 78.

(7) Alain Badiou and Elie During, 'A Theatre of Operations', in *Ibid.* p. 23.

(8) Alain Badiou, 'Theses on Theater', p. 72.

(9) Ian White, 'Performer, Audience, Mirror: Cinema and the Idea of the Live', in *The Sensible Stage: Staging and the Moving Image*, p. 35.

(10) Pil and Galia Kollectiv, 'The Divided Stage: Splitting and the Dialectics of Performance', in *The Sensible Stage: Staging and the Moving Image*, p. 156.

(11) With thanks to Sam Nightingale who suggested this movement from a separation between image and the act or technologies of seeing in *Rear Window* and the conflation of the two in *Hi, Mom!*

(12) Gail Pickering, *Brutalist Premolition* (2008): film and performance. Commissioned by Media Art Bath.

(13) Johan Huizinga, quoted in Eugene Thacker, *In the Dust of This Planet*, p. 56.

Andrew Byrne and Tom Nicholson (2008), *Lines Towards Another Century*: performance documentation, The Elysian Quartet at The Holburne Museum, Bath. Commissioned by Media Art Bath.
Photo: Sam Nightingale.

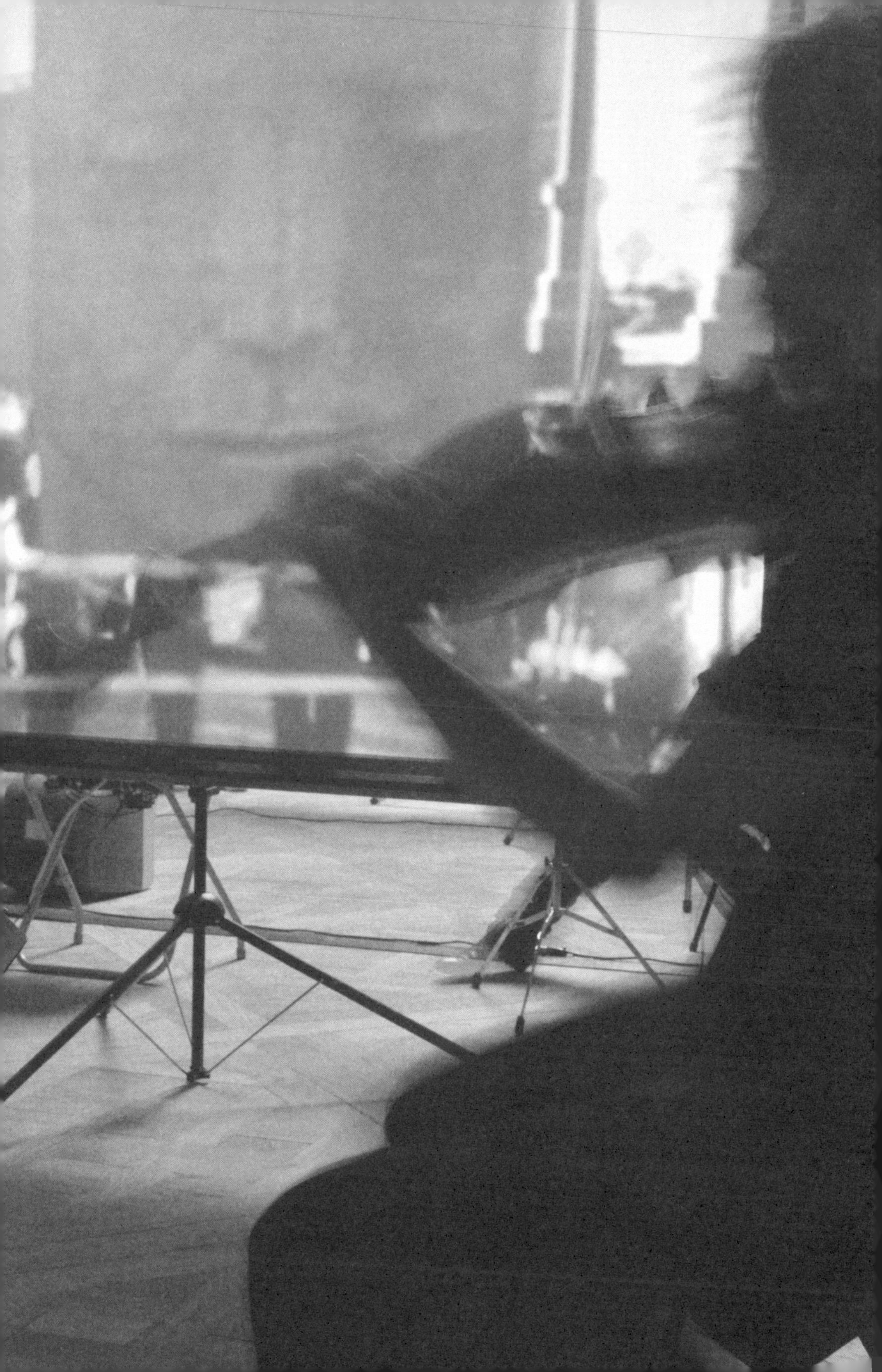

Translated from French by Oliver Feltham.
Reprinted with permission from: *A Theater without Theater*, exhib. cat. (Barcelona and Lisbon: MACBA / Fundaçao de Arte Moderna e Contemporanea and Colecçao Berardo, Lisboa, 2007)

A Theatre of Operations: A Discussion between Alain Badiou and Elie During

ELIE DURING Let's start with a major question. If one grants that a politics of theatre exists, is it possible to speak of a politics of 'theatre without theatre'? A lot has been said about avant-garde theatre abolishing the stage or the separation it implies. In some cases an avant-garde abolished the stage by promoting it as a 'physical concrete site... a unique site without borders or barrier of any sort,' in which the placement of bodies is more important than the text, and which forms 'the theatre of action itself' (Artaud). One can also speak of the abolishing of the auditorium rather than the stage. In any case, what this action marks is the emergence of a new spectator who is no longer a simple spectator but also an actor or actant participating in a kind of collective creation. It is clear that contemporary performance has been heavily influenced by this gesture in the various spaces it constructs whether inside galleries or on their thresholds. But what then remains of the 'public' that is traditionally associated with the idea of theatre? In your opinion, is the suppression of the stage or its transfiguration capable of opening a new space, a site for the emergence of a collective subject?

ALAIN BADIOU The relation between the stage and the public has always been a torturous problem for theatre. Think of Molière's meditations on the duality of the public (the nobles and the bourgeois, the court and the town) or of Brecht's concept of the dialectical division of the audience, of Agit-prop theatre in the Soviet Union, or Vilar's idea of a 'popular' theatre and the vogue of happenings about fifty years ago like the more contemporary fashion of 'street theatre.' In Greece theatre was already a political instrument, or to be exact a function of the State. Wealthy citizens were obliged to pay for theatrical performances through a kind of tax. This is the source of the persistent idea that theatre has a political, democratic and even revolutionary function. In reality, as I have argued ever since my essay 'Rhapsody for the Theatre', theatre is bound to the State; it is a public mediation between the state and its exterior – the crowd, gathered together. And just as circulation occurs in both directions (from power towards the crowd and from the crowd towards power), theatre is entirely ambiguous. It is the point at which a certain audacity of the State encounters the intellectual resources of what is collective, gathered together and public. Louis XIV himself funded Molière's materialist adventures, and in France popular theatre just like street theatre is still funded by the State. I don't think abolishing the stage radically changes this situation. It is merely a formal transformation and the theatre has seen many of those. Why would a crowd which does not revolt against flagrant injustice actually constitute itself as a collective subject through the grace of a theatrical summoning? The ambiguity of the situation of theatre can only continue. Theatre is an art and art will always be a site divided between subversion and institution, contemplative passivity and active rupture, the State and the crowd, creation and the market. An important work displaces these frontiers but it cannot abolish them.

ED But then if the political virtue of theatre resides in its position, the question arises of what remains of that position in performance art. If we define 'theatre without theatre' as a form of pure theatricality, a modality of the presence of bodies freed from representation, performance comes down to the organisation, according to an intention to create art, of an immediate experience of being-together. Consequently is there not a risk that performance will fall into a degraded form of 'ethical' theatre consecrated to revealing either the performativity at work in social exchange or – by staging suffering or mistreated bodies – increasing awareness of the vulnerability of beings and the relation between beings? In fact, just to focus a little, could we return to what constitutes for you the specificity of theatre?

AB I think that there is theatre as soon as there is a public exhibition, with or without a stage, of a desired combination of bodies and languages. The exhibition of the body alone we will name 'dance' and of language alone 'reading,' even if no written text pre-exists. Theatre is the intersection of the two. Moreover it displays elements external to the languages / bodies duality such as images, screens and activities (painting, sculpting or throwing objects, etc.), but these elements simply introduce new dimensions of the body (violence, nudity, sex, imaged deformations, etc.) or of language (soundscapes of all types, mixes of languages, music, etc.). In this framework an insistence on a particular aspect of theatricality, like the contemporary impact on theatre of all the forms of dance or an emphatic use of violence on bodies, would in fact express ideological demands like those you mention: focusing on the fragile life of bodies, on threats to the entirety of what is conceived as 'natural,' hostility to any strict coding of individual life, dissipation of the frontier between public and intimate life, etc.. The problem is that these demands simply reflect contemporary subjectivities rather than presenting a genuine movement for their transformation. What needs to be found – whilst accepting the formal transformations – is a more affirmative element, or rather, to take up Brecht's terms, a didactic element. The question of the relation between theatrical action, performance and politics cannot be reduced to the radicality of gestures. It supposes that all of this be integrated within a larger vision of the challenges of the contemporary epoch.

But before one even gets to that point, perhaps it is not so easy to 'exit' theatre or internally annul it. In fact, theatre cannot be reduced to the stage and its perspective or to the interpretation of a pre-existing given (a text or a protocol for improvisations...). Theatre is a complex ordering system whose material series is not set in stone: texts of course, but also bodies, costumes, the set, the site, music, light... This set is neither closed nor for that matter infinite. But it is in this set that the theatre-Idea must pass; that is, what theatre makes truth out of in the pure present of the material ordering itself. Suppose that someone does nothing more than imperceptibly emphasise everyday gestures to the point of being apparently indiscernible from the 'audience' in which he is operating given that these gestures could just as easily be the 'natural' gestures of an audience member. It would be a case of theatre and not of the absenting of theatre. Why? Because the underlying idea – that every relation to the body can support a performance – can only be transmitted in the present of its material ordering; thus the terrestrial 'passage' of the idea will be coextensive with its immediate activation. It is for exactly the same reason that Duchamp's first ready-mades could not escape the status of the visual arts (painting, sculpture, etc.). In these arts, the passage of the idea is coextensive with the showing of a material form with a contour, however blurred the latter may be. As soon as the display of an indeterminate object can be perceived as the display of the latter's contour, as a local staging of its materiality, the display has a 'plastic' relation to the idea. However an indeterminate corporeal action, once it is grasped as deliberate or 'working,' enters into the 'scenic' arts; it enters dance, mime or theatre. No doubt one could in the end reduce the ideal types of the visual arts (leaving out pure music for the moment) to a transcendental aesthetic. If the displaying gesture that indicates the idea organises the primacy of space (or the contour) over time one has a case of 'plasticity.' If the display organises the evident primacy of time over space, one has 'theatre.' In both cases the subordinate term (time or space) is not suppressed but organised by the other term. I have always seen this in the use of videos as an intervention; whether they are theatrical (incorporated within a display in the present moment, in a slice of time) or 'plastic' (abandoned to their repetitive destiny in a museum room and thus primarily placed in space). The intellectual effect is not the same because the idea that arises in the two cases (if an idea arises) is not presented in identical transcendental systems. So I would quite willingly posit that in principle the most indiscernible performance of everyday gesture remains theatrical in the sense in which Duchamp's readymade remains plastic. When it is a question of determining the artistic register or the formal genre, the gesture and its placement are more important that the exceptional or indeterminate, invented or repeated nature of 'what is' shown by the gesture in its site.

ED To sum up, in what is paradoxically designated as 'theatre without theatre,' the reference to theatre is not merely residual: perhaps it is due to an essential dimension of all performance which is that of thinking in relation if not to a text to be interpreted at least to instructions or statements to be performed, that is, complemented or used as rules which can then be revised. Without such a relation what is it that is performed? What would distinguish performance from the execution of a task in somebody's ordinary life even if that somebody be an artist? The theatre-idea passes via a material ordering which implies statements, even if they be invisible or inaudible. Only in the limit case of the happening with spontaneism is there an aim to emancipate performance from such rules. But it is not because room is made for chance and improvisation that something like an instruction is not implicitly at stake: 'let the party begin!' is still a statement – the zero degree of the script. Between the idea and the act there is the statement. Hence George Brecht's 'events' and some of Allan Kaprow's 'activities' evoke a kind of restricted theatre (in the sense of 'restricted action'). Speech and the text are reduced to instructions or minimal declarations which are not necessarily performatives in the linguist's sense. Could this be compared to Beckett's theatre and his singular montage of gestures and statements?

AB This is an entirely different register, but one of considerable importance. It's a question of knowing whether the theatre of representation has been succeeded or not by a theatre of operations. In more general terms it's a question of whether the display of the theatre-idea ceded its place to the construction of that idea, such that the codes of that construction are themselves visible or shown? In my opinion, the question of the place of ritual, of improvisation, of chance, and that of a spatial relation which is either orientated or not between what is shown and the audience, all of this comes down to discussing – in reference to the most recent experimentation – the relationships between the visible and the invisible in theatrical (or non-theatrical) action.

Here I call 'invisible' the instructions or statements which you rightly identify as being 'between' the idea and the act. For a long time these instructions were half hidden – because they were only present during the rehearsals – or half visible – inasmuch as the Brechtian director wanted to reveal or explain them in the programme. In order to complete the passage from a theatre of display to a theatre of construction (or process) there must definitely be a revision of the nature and place of instructions. The first form of that revision was for just over a century the increasing importance of the director. At the frontier of the visible and the invisible he was the man of instructions (or axioms of performance). Performance, along with the invasion of the stage by schemas drawn from dance or corporeal practices, clearly indicates the end of the century of the director. But that end should in no way be confused with the end of theatre. This is like believing that the end of metaphysical construction in its limited classical schema – implying a theology – is the end of philosophy. The end of the idea of a director of the world is in no way the end of any idea of the world. Theatre has existed for a long time without the separated figure of the director and it will continue without it. The entire question lies in knowing what will then localise the instructions, however random the latter might be. My feeling is that they will become more and more abstract and not corporeal or collective. We are headed, and this is my prophecy, towards an austere theatrical mathematics.

ED Let's enter into the detail of this large scale history: the emergence of a theatre of construction, then of a theatre of process which would seem to find its logical development in the idea of a 'theatre without theatre.' At the turn of the century a revolution occurred in theatre which in a certain way prefigured the turn of visual arts towards performance. You often underline the importance of Meyerhold, and not only for the 'new theatre.' In what manner does Meyerhold form an event for you rather than, say, Stanislavsky? What exactly did he change in the idea of theatre?

AB Stanislavsky, whose work is nevertheless incredibly complex, was mainly interested in what I would call the constructive invariables of theatre: at the center, the construction of the character. The temporal dynamic of the actor is fundamental. As always, the theatre idea is submitted to time, but within a constructive and organised vision of the effects which bring about its manifestation. With Meyerhold it is the collective present which becomes decisive. It is not temporality which is constructive but the artificial display of the present as action. Theatre must primarily indicate how it fuses an active conception of thought with material sequences that frame and exhibit the present as fiction. What's more, the evolution of this fiction has indicated its fragility and division since the active present can just as easily be that of the crucified body, of mystical dialectics (the sublime and the abject), as that of the didactic of choices, of the organised staging of conditions that surround the absolute present of a decision. Indeed, Artaud and Brecht indicate two different ways of being faithful to the Meyerhold event. But in both cases there is performance since no invariant of the type 'character' can be separated from the artifice of a present such as that delivered immediately and collectively by theatre. There is also performance in that all of the tenses of action count equally. We know that for Brecht every scene must be organised according to an energy which makes it comparable to the entire play. Nor can the mystique of cruelty, of the unbearable real, 'expect' the systematic and referential construction to which Stanislavsky was attached. It's true that with Meyerhold the passage of ideas in theatre no longer had to occur via representational mediation. The route was open for performative exercises.

ED These exercises are often described today according to the paradigm of the game: from Wittgenstein's language games to notions of interactivity and participation tied to happenings and media art. It's as though what is expected of games or of play – and yet they have always formed one of the fundamental dimensions of theatre – is that they loosen theatre up... But on the side of the game there is also ceremony and then ritual. Finally there is the feast. How can the theatrical apparatus integrate or evoke these different figures of performance.

AB I believe that theatre has always oscillated between two extremes. On the one hand there is the public taking sides, its commitment, a kind of tendency towards collective fusion whose more or less secret paradigm is the orgy. On the other hand there is the distance and contemplative passivity of a silent and captivated public who attend a ceremony whose paradigm is often celebration, of a religious character. To put it in your terms: the feast and the ritual, or the farce and the tragedy, Aristophanes and Aeschylus; or in the language of the romantic authors, the grotesque and the sublime. When Boileau tells us he does not recognise 'the author of The Misanthrope in the ridiculous sack in which Scapin wraps himself,' he is simply telling us that a genius like Molière circulates freely between the two extremes. Say that it is the sublime of ornamented, statuesque and rarefied bodies that dialectically corresponds to the living abjection of dancing sexed and provocative bodies. Do happenings and new technologies really affect this situation? I don't think so. They introduce new liberties, of course, tied to the contemporary ideology – which is materialistic and democratic. They serve a tendency which I would term vitalist, and which moreover refers in philosophy to Deleuze: performance as a pure immanent becoming opposed to representation or reflection. However, one can easily recognise in this figure the 'orgiastic' tendency present since the very origin.

ED This tendency that you have identified is inseparable from the promotion of the body or of certain dimensions of the body (which could be, if need be, that of the artist-performer, exhibited in its naked presence). Under what conditions can the body be the bearer of new forms and significations?

AB I summed up what I believe to be the dominant ideology today, after the death of God and under the abstract sovereignty of the market, with the formula 'there are only bodies and languages.' The replacement of the space of the stage, which supposes a privileged axis of vision and thus a kind of transcendence, by the immediacy of the body and its nomadic delocalisation is quite simply the artistic projection of that ideology. This projection is quite normal and its consequences must be explored. However it is highly questionable whether it can be seen itself as a subversion or a radical aesthetic because it is first of all, quite simply, an ideological contemporaneity. Here we have a possible milieu for the invention of forms and significations, just as the stage was able to form the possible milieu for the Brechtian rupture but one must not confuse the new sites of invention with the invention itself.

ED Even so, the celebration of the immediacy of the body is not the only orientation in performance. But it is true that representatives of this tendency, Kaprow first in line, primarily reproach theatre for the artificial nature of its apparatus. Of course one can always respond to this by pointing out that artifice is always present in one form or another up to and including the modes of presentation of the performing body. The heritage of pantomime, of the theatre of marionettes, of the Balinese theatre dear to Artaud, of the scenic discipline of Oskar Schlemmer or the biomechanical exercises of Meyerhold is still evident in certain contemporary compositions. With the intervention of prostheses and machines these compositions contradict the celebration of the presence of bodies traversed by Life. In your opinion what is at stake in this reevaluation of artifice as means for art?

AB A crucial question has emerged here. Whatever its site, closed or open, scenic or nomadic, close to or distant from itself, theatre is always a public meditation on the relation or non-relation between artifice and life. Every text in the theory of theatre, from Aristotle to Brecht or Grotowski via Diderot or Meyerhold, deals with this question. The actor or performer is at the centre of this meditation because he or she is the focal point of the conjunction- separation of the two. The actor is the living being who sacrifices, or on the contrary, exhibits vital spontaneity at the service of a collective effect. The problem is always one of either dissimulating artifice under the norm of the natural, or displaying artifice such that the received forms of the natural can be criticised, or showing that any 'nature' is an artificial construction, or even 'naturalising' artifice. I think this last tendency is the most frequently investigated today. The force of technology and its side effects is such that it is tempting to theatricalise it by showing both its prominence and its ultimate defeat via its absorption by life. A kind of monstrous equivalency has been established between vital organs and metallic chimera, thus proposing a new type of unstable equilibrium between artifice and life. Some of David Cronenberg's films explore the same domain in the cinema. In everyday life, piercing is already a kind of local metallisation of flesh. This entire tendency causes a variation in the formula 'there are only bodies and languages': there are only bodies and artifacts. Finally, the philosopher – who generally sees things within a very long temporal span and so distrusts incessant 'novelty' – would say this is all a matter of techne and phusis, there's no way out of it. 'Theatre without theatre' often tries to naturalise artifice by the use of new means under the conditions of technicised democracy. Again, this experimentation is necessary but it says nothing of what it affirms or contests with regard to collective becoming.

ED Let's return for a moment to the politics of performance and to the question of its possible invention of a collective subject. By presenting performance as an act of collective creation Meyerhold broke with a traditional conception of theatre and its capacities which was founded on the formal characteristics of representation. We know that he sometimes invited the public to express themselves directly: in *The Dawn* (1920) and also in the second version of *Mystery Bouffe*. But perhaps he didn't go so far as to introduce the participative relation into the core of theatrical experience. The auditorium was not an appendix tacked on to the stage, however, it wasn't a question of simply fusing these two spaces in order to create an undifferentiated continuum. He defined the auditorium as: 'a workshop of psychophysical energy'...

AB The collective dimension of theatre is essential because the present of the Idea is experienced and investigated through the presence of the public. Theatre is the exemplary artistic form of an immediate liaison between temporal form (the present) and spatial form (the presence of a crowd in a place). The idea of performance, anticipated as it was by Meyerhold and several others throughout the twentieth century (like Agit-prop theatre and its link to revolutionary experiences), consisted in treating this liaison as a shared act, as an indistinction between the time of the idea and the space of the crowd. There must have been something of that kind in the medieval performances of the Passion. The difference lies less in the relationship between the collective and theatrical action than in the existence or not of a compulsory script and the casting of roles. We could perhaps say that performative experience lies at the intersection between the idea of participation, the construction of a new collective, and another requirement of contemporary art; that of the importance of improvisation and openness to chance. A performance is a Passion without a script.

ED This notion of participation joins up with another insistent theme in the history of the avant-gardes: the idea of an art that would no longer present itself as an art but would maintain a relation of continuity with life whilst guarding a capacity for active intervention. Effacing the frontiers between the arts in order to more fundamentally efface the frontiers between art and life: this is what performance attempts to do when it places the physical presence of the performer and the process of performance itself at the heart of the artistic act – grasped as a prolongation of common experience rather than as a staged event or as the construction of an autonomous space. Allan Kaprow reproached Fluxus events precisely for perpetuating the artistic 'framing' of the performance in another form via their maintenance of a minimal script. For Kaprow, contriving a space for the event between the prescriptions of ritual and the chance of improvisation (in which a margin of liberty is opened up by the multiple performances, in varied circumstances, of the same instruction or script) was still giving too much of a role to theatricality. What Kaprow recommended for his part was a kind of 'performance non-art,' freed from any scenic effects, and which can be summarised as developing an attitude, a particular attention to the performative character of everyday tasks (greeting somebody, adjusting one's clothes, etc.).

AB Yes, of course, 'radical' performance is on the side of non-art, of life barely underlined, and without any insistence, as if in passing. This is the most recent form of a desire which goes back, I think, to German romanticism: that it be life itself which is art, that nothing separate the universe of forms from living affirmation, that there be a kind of poem of life. The most recent performative form eliminates even the dimension of poetic enchantment, it establishes itself amidst everyday gestures, in the anything whatsoever, a little like a certain philosophy declares itself the philosophy of 'ordinary language'. I certainly understand that this mythology can be stimulating but I do not share in the enthusiasm for its powers. This mythology already existed in the surrealist and then the situationist interpretation of Rimbaud's existential poetics. Poetry made 'by everyone.' If the 'by everyone' means the promotion of the ordinariness of life to the status of art as non-art I would simply say: even if it is punctuated, the ordinary never delivers anything apart from its vacuity. On this point I hold to a maxim of Antoine Vitez: 'elitist for everyone,' which means: sharing the extraordinary. Whatever its formal destiny may be, art remains a heroic cut out of truth within the resistant material of sense.

ED Chris Burden said: 'It seems that bad art is theatre.' But as you demonstrate it is not so easy to leave theatre. Theatre resists within even the most explicitly 'non-theatrical' forms of performance, which still concentrate whatever remains of 'theatricality' when the text, the stage and even the actor have been subtracted from theatre; in other words, when one has subtracted any form of separation between the director, the 'performer' and the public. But this is precisely the question: what remains? A presence, and also an action or a chain of actions which take place and which are performed at a particular time and place. This execution is more important than the product, the result or end. But what happens in the actual process of performance other than the material inscription of the idea that any body (and any language) can support a performance? Is there something more at stake between this very general idea (that life can and should be performed) and its unique performance each and every time. To make things clearer, perhaps it would be useful to examine the status of the event in performance. People claim that performance renders tangible the taking place of the event. But taking place paradoxically signals a relation to time rather than to space. Space is rather the problem or condition of dance which you describe elsewhere as an art of imminence and restraint and secondarily as an art of the temporal development of movement. Dance is what does not possess a place: what has not yet taken place, or what has already taken place, too soon or too late. On the contrary, the problem of performance, and more particularly the body's exposure in performance in its power of immediate affection, is rather that of wanting to give, if not a show or spectacle, at the very least the integral experience of an event. But is this even possible? Perhaps at this point one should distinguish certain performances which attempt to inscribe the trace of the event, or its irremediably ephemeral character, rather than directly housing its irruption. It would then be less a matter of incarnating the idea formulated by a statement or instruction than that of locally organising, via a play of delays and gaps, the site in which this idea will be unfolded, or the truth that it encloses . . . Here the use of video and every kind of screen, mirror and projection seems to be a crucial resource. Dan Graham's work, at the border between installation and performance, is exemplary. I'm thinking of the form of desynchronisation at work in the deferred video recording of *Present Continuous Past(s)* and in the different versions of *Time Delay*, but equally in the more sober set up of *Past Future Split Attention* in which an anticipated description and a remembered description, an advance and a delay, are articulated within the same space. I would just add that in this case the delay or deferral does not involve any rhetoric of absence, of the absenting or disappearance of gesture, although one can find in it a critique of the ideology of 'live' or 'real time' performance.

AB I think you're quite right there. Performance is the chimera (the 'good' chimera, experimental and interesting) of a 'giving to be seen' of the event. This is why performance is focused on the body; the body drawn out and centered upon its gestural and suffering powers, the body insofar as it is capable of simultaneously declaring the active dimension of the event, its violent surprise, mark or strike, and its passive reception, the effect of subjective transfiguration, the 'pathos' that it can induce. This is also why there is no real contradiction between active violence and the simple discrete generation of traces.

It is of the very essence of the event to be both what irrupts and what solely exists and organises subjects in the form of traces which are immediately difficult to read. One could say that performance takes place precisely between the active force of what emerges and its enigmatic dissemination. Hence one often finds in contemporary performance sudden changes in pace or in the sequencing of, say, cruelty and unconscious tenderness as if they were the same thing. In terms of the event they are actually the same thing. The difference between dance and performance on this point is that dance is a mimetic exposition of the event, an abstraction, and performance on the other hand tries to be a pure indiscernible and tendential real of indeterminate becoming. This is where we find Duchamp again and his structural hesitation between an evident irony and an exemplary seriousness, between the pinnacle of indeterminacy and the pinnacle of sophistication; again as if it were the same thing.

ED Speaking of seriousness and irony, you often insist on the necessity of defining a place for comedy in contemporary theatre. I wonder whether in the domain of performance the burlesque would bear the same charge. Indeed burlesque implies the mastering of an ability that cannot claim any competence or which turns incompetence into a superior competence (Buster Keaton, Chaplin, Peter Sellers). Comedy shares this problem though in the case of burlesque it is generally a matter of a corporeal ability which only becomes linguistic, social or political by extension. It's quite striking how performance art has for the most part cultivated farcical or sordid genres rather than the comic or the burlesque. The burlesque seems to be specific to cinema...

AB There's nothing to add to that excellent remark save that the reason why burlesque triumphed in cinema is that competence-incompetence found an incomparable medium for itself in the mechanisation of movement and the optical illusions that cinema allowed. Méliès is the absolute origin here. In fact we've returned to the initial theme of our discussion: how can technique be integrated into the living peripetia of the body? The cinematographic burlesque was a glorious response to this problem. However, the problem of contemporary comedy is entirely different because it supposes another type of connection. On the one hand there is the incomplete presentation, in the form of a text or any other separable element, of a political Idea in the grand sense: the social and intellectual virtuosity of the lower classes. On the other hand, there is the material combinatory and public element, which completes this idea in the pure present of theatre, which realises its eternity. In the end, comedy is nothing other than the incomparable present of equality, even, I would say, of communism. The classic combinatory was dominated by intrigue, in the double sense of the play's intrigue and the intrigues of the poor, of the young, of women against fathers, the rich, and the old. In the register of farce and sordidness performance is the symptom of the following: how can comedy fulfill its political function (in the final analysis, the people against the State) if the form of the intrigue is out of date? What is a comedy without intrigue? In this line of thought it is definitely Beckett who is still exemplary. Let's say that in the place of comedy with intrigue or plot he substitutes comic sequences, which, moreover, are more theatrical installations than performances. Voices, bodies, becomings, irruptions, are arranged without any plot and yet they indicate the critical power of the indeterminate existent. But language remains, and what language it is! Insofar as theatre is neither dance nor reading, and however performative it might be, everything can disappear from it save language such as it traverses bodies and sites them beyond themselves.

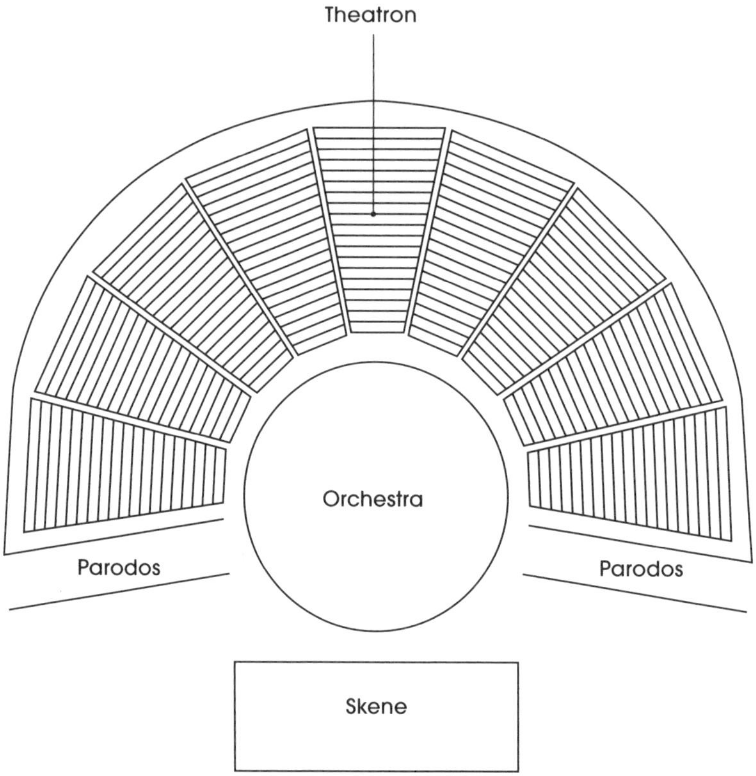

Diagram of a Greek theater

This text is based on two seminar series that I gave in London: *6 or more kinds of theatre*, no.w.here, September to October 2010 and *Performer, Audience, Mirror: Cinema, Theatre and the Idea of the Live*, LUX, September to October 2011. As such I am genuinely indebted to all those who participated in both series and to the generosity and versatility of our conversations, which I aspire to reflect.

Performer, Audience, Mirror: Cinema, Theatre and the Idea of the Live

IAN WHITE

The body is a false promise. To be lifelike is not to live. Or, liveness (liveness) is not life*like*ness. Just because somebody is actually there, a body on a stage is no more of a guarantee that what we are seeing is categorically live than an emotion portrayed by an actor on the screen is an indication that something was actually felt, even though we might think they are these things. Cinema is not live by definition. The same 'film' is played every time. A theatre play might require bodies but the actor is as controlled by the mechanisation of rehearsal and repetition as the 'moving' image. Even if it is not seen as such, the same hand moves to the same place, at the same angle, through the same axis at every performance.

By plotting the ways in which neither cinema nor theatre are live, I want then to consider exactly the opposite proposition: that in thinking cinema and theatre together, they might be the means by which liveness could be further described both as, and not only as, the product of an extraordinary kind of negation, and to indicate what has been or might be at stake by doing so.

ONE (CINEMA)

Two people face each other. One speaks a line to the other: 'I love you', for example. The person opposite repeats it, inverted from the first to the second person:

'You love me'.

One: 'I love you'.

Two: 'You love me' and so on.

Each time the person speaking inflects the phrase with a different emotional nuance: tenderness, defiance, desperation, horror, declaration, surprise, rhetoric, disbelief, question, accusation and so on. A linguistic face-off until one person cracks or changes tack, what seems like a game is actually a popular training exercise for actors devised by Sanford Meisner. It is also an accumulation of incremental non-responses or an absolutely, repetitively constructed and incrementally evacuated present for the sake of portraying an emotional truth, or Truth itself: what Meisner might call the means for *Living Truthfully Under Imaginary Circumstances,* by which he means acting defined as re-action rather than agency, and proposed as a worry-free suspended state of happiness, which is also the title of an exhibition by Anja
fig. 4 __ Kirschner and David Panos. The artwork maps such exercises and contextualises them with documentary material and a showreel of actors in Hollywood feature films deploying their learning. Emanating from two experiences of loss – the death of his brother and the economic crash of the 1930s that led to World War II – Meisner's technique is proposed as both the product of and a palliative for the moment in which it was conceived. Reframed in this work it becomes a metaphor for the artists' own reading of a state of contemporary crisis. The dividing lines (is/is not, have/have not) usually marked by the difference between spectator and representation, the self and another and between subject and object are collapsed, embodied here as both a practice and a theory of acting. Or as a depoliticised state of in-action and in-conclusion, of participants and spectators subjugated in/by capitalism as image-play. The work echoes Dan Graham's analysis of the consumer constructed by a shop window, through a window that is also a screen, seeing their own face reflected, superimposed onto a commodity, indivisible from the empty, cold field of glass that purposefully flattens and contains (becomes) them both: 'Inseparable from the goods the consumer desires is the illusion that buying them will "complete" that which is "incomplete" in himself. This desire is never satisfied (as the market system must continue to function)...' (1)

TWO (THEATRE)

> *Your sensation as one in the audience in relation to the play played before you your sensation I say your emotion concerning that play is always either behind or ahead of the play at which you are looking... your emotion as a member of the audience is never going on at the same time as the action of the play. This thing... is what makes one endlessly troubled about a play*
>
> __ Gertrude Stein, 'Plays' (2)

Considered as a picture, the stage of a proscenium theatre functions according to the principles of Renaissance perspective. Like the lines that can be drawn from the central figures of Plato and Aristotle in Raphael's fresco *The School of Athens* (1510-11), in the theatre, power emanates from the focal point of the presented image to the audience by virtue of the fact that it organises or re-orders – distorts, constructs – space, bodies (in the picture and of its surroundings) and time. And emotion. This power persuades and our nervousness in the face of it is what Stein describes as the symptom of its endless trouble – the nag of our own lack and our repeated, frustrated attempts to catch up, to enter, to be fulfilled by. The contemporary theatre maker Robert Wilson organises his stage as a picture designed and choreographed to be viewed from the middle of the stalls (from where it was directed) for optimal impact, that is, greatest visual pleasure, or less 'trouble'. And so sitting at the back of the auditorium, on the end of a row – in a cheap seat – throws the picture into radical relief. The power structure breaks down because the lines of persuasion effected by perspective are broken. A swivelled picture plain reveals the apparatus of the work like exposed cogs in the back of an analogue watch, a mechanism that does not tell us the time but measures it.

A fixed perspective inscribing time – not its machinery (the timeline of history) – is the metaphor deployed by the artist Lis Rhodes in her essay for the Hayward Gallery exhibition *Film As Film* (1979):

> *...history represented... is the illusion of a philosophical ideal, the meshing of moments to prove a theoretical connection. It is though a line could be drawn between past and present and pieces of a person's life and work pegged on it... an inflexible chain, each part in place. The pattern is defined. Cut the line and chronology falls in a crumpled heap. I prefer a crumpled heap, history at my feet, not stretched above my head.* (3)

Perspective is there, too, in shop windows. Dan Graham:

> *The showcase window as a framing or optical device replicates the form of the Renaissance painting's illusion-ary, three-dimensional 'space'. Like a painting's perspective, it frames a determined view (determines a view), creating a point of focus – meaning – organised around a central vanishing point. The customer's gaze is focused upon the centered object's external form; focus creates value.* (4)

The conditions of the 'not-live' of both cinema and theatre infect each other along the axis of the architecture of reception and its history that they also share and of which they are also an aesthetic, economic, critical and political function: the auditorium.

THREE (THE IDEA OF THE LIVE)

If the auditorium – definitively idealised (realised), let us say, in Wagner's opera house at Bayreuth in Germany since 1876 as a perfect, 'pure' space for total immersion (sound, light, image: invisible apparatus) – functions against a construction of liveness, the obvious and easiest way to initiate its reintroduction would be to remove this architecture and its paradigms as a possible location. The history of performance art is often read as such. Positioned most recently by Claire Bishop as a de- or re-skilled subset of theatre where the proximity between performer and audience is recalibrated (intensified) by the same-time, same-place effect of the fully lit white cube of the gallery space which replaces the immersive, black box of the divided theatrical auditorium (lit stage, darkened auditorium), it is also characterised by a rejection of virtuosic display that accompanied such a shift. But might not the theatrical auditorium also be a location for the same mobilisation of desire that Bishop ascribes to de-skilled performances? (5)

Leaving aside an argument based on reading experimental film as a subset of industrial ('Hollywood') cinema as proof of its coincidence with performance art as a subset of theatre (their similar histories, entering into the discourses of contemporary art via a challenge to the institution by the politics of the dematerialised art object and conceptual practices of the post-happenings, film-co-op-spawning Golden Age of the late 1960s and 70s) the auditorium becomes a productive limit or a dialectical location containing all the potential of a crumpled heap. Far from being eliminated it is the function by which a set of terms are generated, however wildly, that pertain to the live, peculiarly defined as the product of a cross-feed between cinema and theatre, proposing, however perversely, a certain kind of cinema *as* live. What then is liveness? Where do we find it?

Before cinema assumed the fully industrialised form in which we receive it today (in the form of a post-Wagnerian *dispositif*) early descriptions of what happened there – its potential – differ significantly from those of the subjected, gendered, manipulated or disciplined bodies of its audience. Consider, for example, the cinema reportage of Dorothy Richardson's column 'Continuous *Performance*' (emphasis mine) in 1928:

> *...here we are and there she is. In she comes and the screen obediently ceases to exist. If when finally she attends to it – for there is first her toilet to think of, and then her companion, perhaps not seen since yesterday – she is disappointed, we all hear of it... her conversation proceeds uninterrupted. And to this we do not entirely object.*
>
> *...all her bad manners that will doubtless be pruned when the film becomes high art and its temple a temple of stillness save for the music that at present inspires her to do her worst, she is innocently, directly, albeit unconsciously, upon the path that men have reached through long centuries of effort and of thought. She does not need, this type of woman clearly does not need, the illusions of art to come to the assistance of her own sense of existing. Instinctively she maintains a balance, the thing perceived and herself perceiving... She takes all things currently. Free from man's pitiful illusion of history, she sees everything in terms of life... [she] testifies that life goes on, art or no art and that the onlooker is a part of the spectacle.*(6)

Richardson had more aspirations for this new situation: 'Cinema... is a medium, or a weapon... The new film can, at need, assist radio in turning the world into a vast council chamber...'(7) She answers, a few months prior, Bertolt Brecht's frustrated desire for that other medium: 'As for the radio, I don't think it can consist merely in bringing back cosiness to the home and making family life bearable again. But quite apart from its dubious functions, radio is one-sided when it should be two.' Richardson echoes Brecht's suggestion to: 'change this apparatus over from distribution to communication... to receive as well as to transmit... to let the listener speak as well as hear... [to] bring him [sic] into a relationship... [to] step out of the supply business and organise its listeners as suppliers...'(8) And this is a sentiment no less reflected by his own model of a new type of theatre to replace 'the theatre as we know it [which] shows the structure of society (represented on the stage) as incapable of being influenced by society (in the auditorium)' with one 'which not only releases the feelings, insights and impulses possible within the particular historical field of human relations in which the action takes place but employs and encourages those thoughts and feelings which help transform the field itself.'(9) And it is this model of theatre that informs Peter Gidal's *Theory and Definition of Structural / Materialist Film*, perhaps also, now, the model of a cinema:

> *Structural/Materialist film attempts to be non-illusionist. The process of the film's making deals with devices that result in demystification or attempted demystification of the film process... In Structural/Materialist film, the in/film (not in/frame) and film/viewer material relations, and the relations of the film's structure are primary to any representational content.*(10)

Read, then (again), Alain Badiou, summarising the 'collective dimension of theatre' during the introductory conversation to the exhibition *A Theatre Without Theatre* (MACBA, 2007) that is also contained in this book:

> *Theatre is the exemplary artistic form of an immediate liaison between temporal form (the present) and spatial form (the presence of a crowd in a place). The idea of performance, anticipated as it was by Meyerhold and several others throughout the twentieth century (like Agit-prop theatre and its link to revolutionary experiences), consisted in treating this liaison as a shared act, as an indistinction between the time of the idea and the space of the crowd... the intersection between the idea of participation, the construction of a new collective, and another requirement of contemporary art; that of the importance of improvisation and openness to chance.*(11)

Badiou's theatre and *a particular kind* of cinema are constituted as a political threat. Not because of the power of persuasion implemented by an architecture of control but because of a capacity for facilitating instability, that is, a shared world creation predicated not on the evacuated, depoliticised present represented by *narrative* cinema but by the construction of an immediate, inevitably politicised, unstable present in which, as a matter of form, of a form in use, viewers are complicit as Badiou suggests. Dan Graham describes such complicity as the property of another medium also – video:

> *Video is a present-time medium. Its image can be simultaneous with its perception by/of its audience (it can be the image of its audience perceiving). The space/time it presents is continuous, unbroken, and congruent with that of the real time which is the shared time of its perceivers and their individual and collective real environments... In a live-video-situation, the spectator may be included within the frame at one moment, or be out of the frame at another moment... video feeds back...*(12)

The model then for this model of the complicity of video (cinema, theatre) as a feedback loop with political potential is located by William Kaizen in yet another medium: television – in spite of its ideological operations – *because* its template is an idea of the live.

Video, Kaizen argues, was always already coded as 'live' because of its use in broadcast television and that, since its inception in the 1950s, television generated: 'its reality effect from always seeming to be live because it always opens onto the possibility of continuous live transmission... even when not live, television seems live...'(13) He continues: 'in live television, no matter how carefully scripted or composed the presentation, the threat of disaster lurks.'(14)

> *[I]t is as if it [television – etymologically 'far-seeing', tele-vision, bringing something far away close-to] were a window that tunnelled through to another place, opening directly onto the event shown. In this it is closer, both rhetorically and technically, to the present tense of theatre than to film.*(15)

The event shown is in the room. And the room is in the event shown. At which point a material hallucination under pressure of which those perspective lines of the proscenium theatre are radically re-imagined, their function challenged and reconstituted... Imagine for example, a diagram of the Greek amphitheatre. It looks like a fan, the pivot of which is the circular stage surrounded by its banks of grandstand seating that span out around it. In the diagram, the steps by which the seats are accessed are radial struts, their fulcrum the middle of the circular stage. Read (backwards) from the perspective of the Renaissance, the centre of the circular stage, in diagram form, is revealed as a focal point. It is the vanishing point of the lines of perspective into which the bodies of spectators are themselves organised by the architecture of their seating in relation to the stage. Such an arrangement might subject an audience to the power of persuasion, of the story being told, but the story was often already known, perspective as an optical device was not, the stage is not framed like a picture but experienced as a 'perspective' field in which the audience is actually also sat, able to see the actors and also each other. The time and space of the auditorium extends into that of what is being shown, it is organised into it, not reorganised by it. Performer, audience, mirror.

This diagram we have imagined is mirrored in the auditoria of the Baroque: you are sat inside a box in the dress circle of the theatre; your own curtain is swept back along the lines of the arch that frames the front of your box, your view. This view almost exactly replicates the proscenium arch of the stage, its own curtain swept back to reveal an on-stage architecture that repeats the stone columns of the auditorium that also frame it, illusorily diminishing in size to a vanishing point the lines of which extend directly from you, uninterrupted, let us say, into the stage-space to an imaginary focal point, at an impossible distance away that is also absolutely present as if you yourself have been tunnelled through space and time or what is shown tunnels to you – subject of an immediate present. And you realise that actually you are sat inside an eighteenth century feedback loop that comes from materialist film, and/or (strange, I know) video, via television, as cinema, in the theatre. Like it, you are live.

But I digress. I've made this reading up, based on a diagram I saw of a Greek amphitheatre and a photograph of the finest of one of Europe's few remaining Baroque theatres at the Český Krumlov Palace in the Czech Republic. But my fantasy is not one of Wagnerian total immersion. It is a model of complicity that is thrown into relief, with revealing irony, by another altogether more strict model of a cinema – an actual auditorium that did once exist: Peter Kubelka's *Invisible Cinema* designed by the filmmaker as the first auditorium of Anthology Film Archives in New York, is instructive here for what it mitigates against.

The *Invisible Cinema* is well documented and railed against as being disciplinarian. It was intentionally so. A pure black box where the only light source is the screen itself, spectators were separated from one another by panels dividing their seats at eye level like blinkers so that only the screen could be seen. It is anticipated as a structure by the early French theorist Jean Goudal's description of the ideal auditorium as a place where:

> *Our problems evaporate, our neighbours disappear. Our body itself submits to a sort of temporary depersonalisation which takes away the feeling of its own existence... the darkness of the auditorium destroys the rivalry of real images that would contradict the ones on the screen.*(16)

If we bristle at the reported austerity of this space, or if this room seemed out of step with other developments in experimental film of the time – in particular the practice of expanded cinema – then Kubelka makes its purpose clear:

> *This kind of cinema is not for multimedia, multi-screen, multiple speakers or for live action mixed with film... There is nothing really radical in this project, this is normal cinema.*(17)

> *If it looks different, it's because other theatres are abnormal. They are like living rooms equipped with huge television sets.*(18)

By this Kulbelka means, I think, that the television set in a living room is seen in a context and watched inattentively – a lack of attention that John Berger alternatively seeks to rectify in episode one of his 1972 BBC television series on art and its mediation, *Ways of Seeing*, by addressing the viewer directly:

> *Botticelli's Venus and Mars used to be a unique image which it was only possible to see in the room where it was actually hanging. Now its image [by television]... can be seen in a million different places at the same time. As you look at [these images] now, on your screen, your wallpaper is round them, your window is opposite them, your carpet is below them. At this same moment they are on many other screens surrounded by different objects, different colours, different sounds. You are seeing them in the context of your own life. They are surrounded not by gilt frames but by the familiarity of the room you are in and the people around you.*(19)

Whether we like it or not, the *Invisible Cinema* is, for sure, no feedback loop; and it is not for the kind of cinema that we now call expanded, a practice more literally live than my own assisted speculations about the auditorium. By implication expanded cinema could be defined also as the set of things that the *Invisible Cinema* is not: abnormal, social, physical, personal-political, a room (not a screen), with visible apparatus and operators, plural (multimedia, multi-speakers), a situation of live action and a (Marxist!) television set.

What Dan Graham writes about video and William Kaizen of its template, television, becomes exemplary in this regard. Therefore, expanded cinema could be considered as a practice that extends or multiplies the frame of the screen to incorporate what is happening in the screening room itself, to include space, movement, live speaking, to incorporate the corporeality of the spectator as also constituting the work itself through relative, physical positions in space. Perhaps a literally moving image, an artwork that is contingent upon the instability of performance and meaning that is constituted more by a multifaceted response mediated by these things than visual reception alone, expanded cinema might also be figured as a special case of the feedback loop in which the viewer becomes multiply complicit: complicit because the viewer (the receiver of this work) is also one of the work's prime agents, or actors. Regarded as such – as a medium defined by the limit of the auditorium that it functions against – expanded cinema finds its own apotheosis in the work of art as an instruction, where the frame of the work is multiplied and extended not only into the room where the work is viewed but also disintegrating these physical limits to occupy the world at large – life, itself, material.

There is no clearer an example of this than the work of Orders & Co. that Mike Sperlinger describes in his essay, 'Orders! Conceptual Art's Imperatives'. Orders & Co. sent a series of cards to the President of Uruguay in 1971 that co-opted him, irrespective of his will, into unavoidably performing a work that simultaneously inverted both a separation between art and life and the usual: 'relationship between orderers and those ordered, breaking the vicious circle of power.'[20] The only surviving evidence of these instructions is collected in Lucy Lippard's source book, *Six years: The dematerialisation of the art object from 1966 to 1972...*, no primary documents exist:

> *Oct 5: Our next order is for the 15th of October. That day you will take special care to button your pants before going out into the street. Oct 30: The 5th of November you will simulate normal walking but you will be conscious that for this day Orders & Co. have taken possession of every third step you take. It is not necessary to obsess yourself with this.*[21]

Sperlinger argues that the instruction work, characterised in part as a 'rhetoric of withdrawal,' with all the paradoxes that an artwork based on such terms confronts, finds its 'limit-case' in Lee Lozano's *General Strike Piece, Feb. 8th, 1969* (1969):

> *Gradually but determinedly avoid being present at official or public 'uptown' functions or gatherings related to the 'art world' in order to pursue investigation of total personal & public revolution. Exhibit in public only pieces which further sharing of ideas and information related to total personal & public revolution. In process at least through summer, '69.*[22]

FOUR (_____)

The body is a promise. Removing it – its *like*ness – is a political act. Political cinema, political theatre are live. What is this –

LIVENESS?

MATERIAL
ACCIDENT
SIMULTANEITY
DISRUPTION
DISORDER
THREAT
COMMUNITY
PROVISIONAL COMMUNITY
VIDEO
FEEDBACK LOOP
VIDEO RADIO
VIDEO RADIO CINEMA
VIDEO RADIO CINEMA TELEVISION
THEATRE
POSSIBILITY
RADIO CINEMA TELEVISION
IMMEDIACY
CINEMA TELEVISION
ABNORMAL
TELEVISION
SOCIAL
PHYSICAL
PERSONAL
EXISTENCE
SPACE
VISIBLE
REALITY
PLURAL
ACTION
IMMATERIAL
THEATRICAL

WITHDRAWAL.

ENDNOTES

(1) Dan Graham, 'Essay on Video, Architecture, and Television', in *Two-way Mirror Power: Selected Writings by Dan Graham on His Art*, ed. Alexander Alberro (Cambridge, Massachusetts & London: The MIT Press, 1999), pp. 57-8.

(2) Gertrude Stein, 'Plays', *Look at Me Now and Here I am: Writing and Lectures, 1909-45*, ed. Patricia Meyerowitz (London: Peter Owen Publishers, first published 1967, republished 2004), p. 59.

(3) Lis Rhodes, 'Whose History?', in *Film as Film: Formal Experiment in Film 1910-75*, exhibition catalogue (London: Hayward Gallery, 1979), pp. 119-120.

(4) Dan Graham, 'Essay on Video, Architecture, and Television', p. 58.

(5) 'In the U.S. in the late 1950s, performance art... took place in the actual space-time of the viewer, and these contingencies of location and audience were often factored into the work. The incontrovertible frisson of real life was the steering principle; no suspension of disbelief was necessary because everything was purportedly "real."' / '...the best forms of de-skilling evoke in the viewer something of ... spectralisation: Such works generate in us not a disdainful "I could do that" but the generative energy of "I want to do that!"', Claire Bishop, 'Unhappy Days in the Art World', published online in *The Brooklyn Rail: Critical Perspectives on Arts, Politics and Culture*: http://www.brooklynrail.org/2011/12/art/unhappy-days-in-the-art-worldde-skilling-theater-re-skilling-performance.

(6) Dorothy Richardson, 'Continuous Performance VIII', in *Close Up*, Vol. II, no. 3, March 1928, reprinted in *Close Up, 1927-33: Cinema and Modernism*, ed. James Donald, Anne Friedberg, Laura Marcus (Princeton, New Jersey: Princeton University Press & London: Cassell: London, 1998), pp. 175-6.

(7) 'Continuous Performance: The Film Gone Male', *Close Up*, Vol. IX, no.1, March 1932, reprinted in *Close Up, 1927-33: Cinema and Modernism*, ed. James Donald, Anne Friedberg, Laura Marcus (Princeton, New Jersey: Princeton University Press & London: Cassell: London, 1998), p. 207.

(8) Bertolt Brecht, 'The Radio as an Apparatus of Communication', 'Der Rundfunk als Kommunikationsapparat', *Blätter des Hessischen Landestheaters*, Darmstadt, no. 16, July 1932, reprinted in *Brecht on Theatre: The Development of an Aesthetic*, ed. John Willett (Methuen: London, 1964), p. 52.

(9) Bertolt Brecht, '*A Short Organum for the Theatre*' , parts 33 & 35, 'Kleines Organon für das Theater' in *Sinn und Form, Sonderheft Bertolt Brecht*, Potsdam, 1949, reprinted in *Brecht on Theatre: The Development of an Aesthetic*, ed. John Willett (Methuen: London, 1964), pp. 189 & 190.

(10) Peter Gidal, 'Theory and Definition of Structural/Materialist Film', in *Structural Film Anthology*, ed. Peter Gidal (London: British Film Institute, 1976), p. 1.

(11) See pp. 17-29: 'A Theatre of Operations, A Discussion Between Alain Badiou and Elie During', first published in *A Theater Without Theater*, exhibition catalogue (Barcelona: Museu d'Art Contemporani de Barcelona & Lisbon: Fundação de Arte Moderna e Contemporânea - Colecção Berardo, 2007), p. 25.

(12) Dan Graham, 'Essay on Video, Architecture, and Television', p. 52.

(13) William Kaizen, 'Live on Tape: Video, Liveness and the Immediate', in *Art and the Moving Image: A Critical Reader*, ed. Tanya Leighton (London: Tate Publishing & Afterall, 2008), p. 264.

(14) *Ibid.* p. 262.

(15) *Ibid.* pp. 263-4.

(16) Jean Goudal, 'Surrealism and Cinema', 1925. Quoted in Noam M. Elcott, 'On Cinematic Invisibility: Expanded Cinema Between Wagner and Television', in *Expanded Cinema: Art, Performance and Film*, ed. A. L. Rees, David Curtis, Duncan White, Steven Ball (London: Tate Publishing, 2011), p.44.

(17) Peter Kubelka, *Design Quarterly*, no. 93, 1974.

(18) Peter Kubelka quoted in *New York Times*, 29 November 1970.

(19) Author's own transcription from the television programme.

(20) From a letter accompanying the copies of Orders & Co.'s instructions sent to Lucy Lippard, quoted in Mike Sperlinger, 'Orders! Conceptual Art's Imperatives' in *afterthought: new writing on conceptual art*, ed. Mike Sperlinger (London: Rachmaninoff's, 2005), p. 1.

(21) Quoted in *Ibid.*, p. 2.

(22) Quoted in *Ibid.*, p. 19.

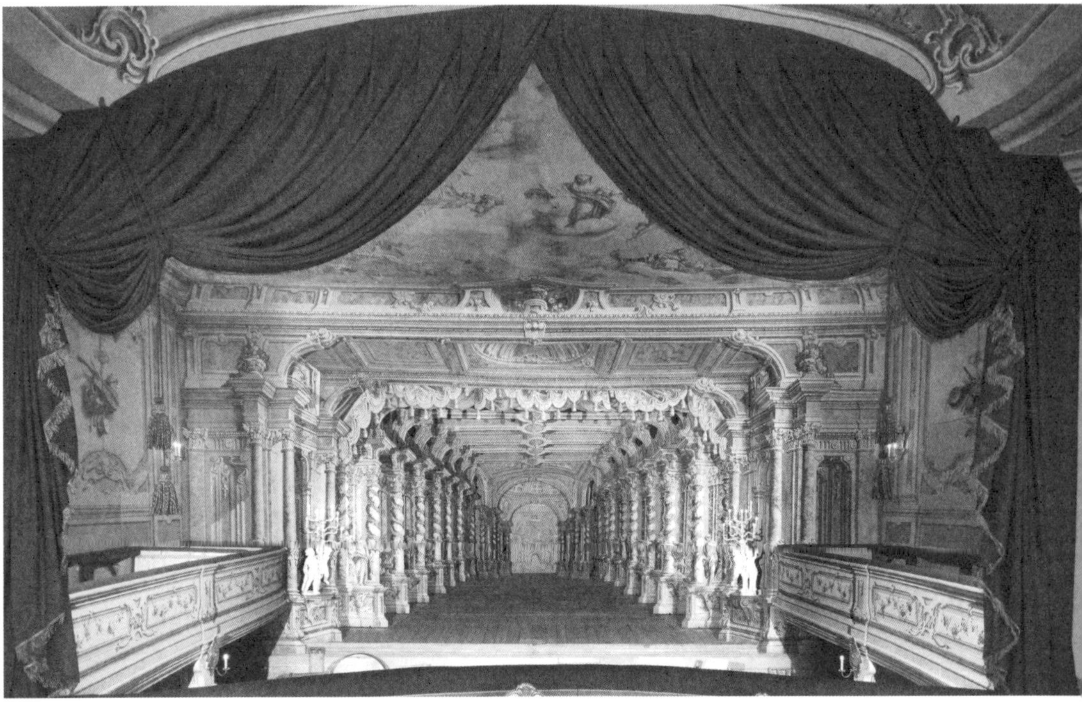

Český Krumlov Baroque Theatre, image courtesy Czech Tourist Authority (photo.czechtourism.com).

Marguerite Duras, 'Je suis photographe', les Cahiers du cinéma, Hors Série 20, Avril 1997. In this article, Marguerite Duras comments on the film *Blow Up* by Michelangelo Antonioni, which powerfully evokes the ambivalent relationship between narrative and photography, and between the mechanical eye of the camera and the photographer's agency.

'Je suis photographe': Figures of Cinematic Narrators

VANESSA DESCLAUX

> *The prints unknowingly reproduce images that belong to history but keep repeating themselves; the appearance of the grain of the paper is endlessly bound to miracle, capable of trapping murderous couples in their flight, time and time again.*
>
> __ Marcelline Delbecq, *Des impressions, des ombres* (1)

In the vast spectrum of work that cinema has been in a process of unfolding since its beginning, the relation between sounds, words and images has proven to construct very different types of spaces and temporalities. The works in dialogue in this essay find ways to question the nature of movement in film, and more particularly the tension between still images and moving images in the production of time. They imagine new configurations to confront words and images, thus producing new forms of narratives and new modes of narrating. Marc Camille Chaimowicz, Charlotte Moth and Marcelline Delbecq do not define themselves as filmmakers: their field of work is certainly the visual arts, yet their practices directly or indirectly refer to seminal, though often marginal, figures in the field of cinema such as Marguerite Duras, Chris Marker or Hollis Frampton. Duras appears of paramount importance here because it is through her unique oeuvre that the question of the performative dimension of such moving image productions is the most relevant. In Duras' works indeed, the figure of the narrator, whose voice unfolds over the images, shows two specific traits: on the one hand, this voice proposes a literary experience, it is the voice of the reader of a written text, and on the other hand, this voice is embodied – even when Duras does not appear on screen, which is actually very rare – and personified, letting this voice move between the figure of the author, the figure of a character and the more metonymic figure of both love and desire. If Delbecq and Moth have sometimes put aside the voice-over in favour of written text on the screen – as is the case in Moth's *Absent Forms* (2011) and Delbecq's *Eden* (2011) – the literary experience displaces the figure of the reader to the spectator, and recalls the experience of the early twentieth century silent cinema, to which they often refer to in their work.

If performance is traditionally associated with acting in the field of cinema, we face here a radically different kind of gesture and action. 'Performance', in the works that I will discuss, pertains to the activity of the voice in giving form to a text. The notion of performance might also be associated with other events that concur in configuring – or we might say in certain instances 'disfiguring' – the relations between sound, words, movement and images in the context of the works by filmmakers and artists such as Duras and Chaimowicz as well as Moth.

Duras's film, *Le Camion* (1977) alternates two different shots – one shows a lorry moving through the industrial countryside of the Paris region, while the other records a conversation between the actor Gérard Depardieu and Duras herself. In her home studio, which Duras calls 'La chambre noire' (the dark room), they read the script, written in the conditional tense, of a possible film about 'the lady of the lorry'. Last year, Chaimowicz shot various scenes in a seventeenth century chateau in Burgundy, involving three young women who indifferently embody the three female characters of Jean Genet's 1947 play, *The Maids.* Chaimowicz fragmented the shoot and future edits into a series of staged gestures and postures – some directly recalling moments in the text – and into readings of chosen fragments of the play, often letting the female voices overlap, speaking in both English and French. He allowed the immobile camera to record the events as they unfolded while he focused his attention on looking through a still camera to take photographs. The resulting film, weaving together fragments of filmed sequences and still images, *The Casting of The Maids,* was presented as a first cut in Norwich (UK) in April 2011. Chaimowicz's *The Casting of The Maids* and Marguerite Duras' *Le Camion* both propose a staging of the act of reading, making manifest the desire to read the text rather than perform it. These two works strip down the cinematic apparatus and reduce as much as possible the distance between the text and its representation.

In his seminal film *(nostalgia)* (1971), Hollis Frampton looks back at a series of photographs that he took in New York throughout the 1960s. And we too engage in the act of looking at these images, one by one, while the disembodied voice of a narrator comments on the images. Yet what the voice describes does not immediately seem to be what we see because Frampton introduces a time-lapse between the image on screen and the image that is narrated. In her book, *Hollis Frampton (nostalgia)*, Rachel Moore describes the work in these terms:

> *The action is confined to a hot plate on which photographs lie and then proceed to combust. The narration is a series of musings about the photographs. Despite such confinement the film nonetheless takes us on a trip of sorts, from past to present, from silence to language and from photography to film.*[2]

Through the desynchronising of narrative and image, while introducing movement through the means of fire, Frampton immediately takes the images outside of the linearity of historical time and makes them disappear in the present of the act of seeing and listening. Frampton plays with the temporality proper to cinema, positioning the spectator in a constant flow between remembering and anticipating. The temporal construction of the film – 24 frames per second – confronts itself to the different temporality of cinematic narration, slowed down by Frampton to a point of stillness through its focus on frozen photographs, condemned one by one to destruction on the hot plate. Through this work, Frampton makes palpable the conflicted relationship between the inescapable movement of time in film and the intense stillness of photographic images. As Moore then adds: 'The ability to take hold of the image, to contemplate it alone, endlessly, to see it in the light, trade off for the risk, contingency and sheer plasticity of time this nerve-wracking medium propels.'[3]

Frampton brings forth his cinematic construction by means of the gradual disappearance of his photographic archive, producing movement through combustion and driving the narrative irreparably forward by erasing the evidence of the past. Moth has built her own archive of photographs, *Travelogue* (1999-), as 'an organic thought process, a collage', which she constantly revisits and expands through different travels connected to research and exhibition projects.[4] Various modes of editing and display have made these photographs manifest, enhancing their anonymous and ahistorical character, as another mode of disappearance. Caroline Hancock has described the spaces captured by Moth as 'the land of disco balls, ice cream cones, multicoloured balloons and sequined curtains', stressing Moth's particular interest in: 'vernacular as well as grand architecture or the spaces in-between... timeless spaces of everyday banality.'[5] Part of an endless conceptual activity, Moth's Travelogue is at once autobiographical and a mute accumulation of images that remains entirely open to the viewer's own narrative projections, and although often presented in three-dimensional configurations that unfold images in space, Moth's infinite archive demonstrates her affinity with Frampton's conception of time in cinema. Frampton writes:

> *Time in cinema is precisely as plastic, malleable, tactile as the physical substance of film itself. Plastic to a point that comes down to a bedrock when one puts up against the frame only twenty-four frame per second. When it comes to that [time] becomes rigid, though it can be compressed, attenuated. There is also something that is plastic, malleable, that is, if you will, tactile. The divisions go far past a twenty-fourth of a second and this, of course, is the vast organism, which passes through all of us and through which we pass, called consciousness. The consciousness of the passing of time, the density, the sense that something will happen, that nothing will happen.*[(6)]

Marcelline Delbecq has repeatedly taken hold of a unique image, letting the spectator contemplate that image alone. Delbecq gives a central position to photography, which she uses to expose some of her spoken narratives, voice-over soundtracks that accompany the viewer/listener throughout a journey into a photographic image, either as photographic print (*Oblivion*, 2009; *Daleko*, 2008) or
fig. 5 __ light box (*Rapture*, 2007) hung on the wall of the exhibition space. Each of these works displays one single image. The sound recording that rolls over (writes over) the image is of varying lengths, not very long but much longer than the time a visitor would normally spend in front of a single picture in an exhibition. What came first – text or image – might be matter for question as the relationship between narrative and photograph is not of objective commentary or visual description:

> *The audible presents fluidity, passing, a certain inchoate, amorphous character, and a lack of distance. The voice is elusive, always changing, becoming, elapsing, with unclear contours, as opposed to the relative permanence, solidity, durability of the seen... It deprives us of distance and autonomy. If we want to localize it, to establish a safety distance from it, we need to use the visible as the reference.*[(7)]

The image might thus provide this margin of distance and autonomy, which prevents the listener from letting his thoughts drift away. The photograph might play the role of perspective in classical painting: it gives a structure, a guide to reading, or in Delbecq's instance, listening. In Delbecq's works, the image produces an encounter with the voice as a point of shared understanding, while offering the rest of the distance that separates them as an indeterminate space to explore visually as much as in a literary manner. Despite the similarities of the three aforementioned *dispositifs* (*Oblivion*, *Daleko* and *Rapture*), the three situations appear dramatically different in their details. None of the works stage a similar relationship between words and image: if *Rapture* creates a radical gap between the visual and its narrative counterpart, with no elements letting the two spaces overlap, *Daleko* unfolds a view of a specific landscape through both photograph and narrative. In *Oblivion*, the image in the photograph is unveiled at the very end of the narrative, positioning the listener in a similar wander as the character throughout the story.

The single image does not function as a complete representation but rather as a fragment, a blurred snapshot, and an unstable memory. Delbecq's way of working from a single image allows her nonetheless to deploy a cinematic approach to image making and narration. As Jacques Rancière stresses:

> *[Cinematic modernity] opposes to the narrative or signifying relations between images of classic cinema, an autonomous power of the image that would mark itself twice: through an autonomous temporality and through the void that separates it from others.*[8]

This autonomous power of the image is demonstrated in Delbecq's *dispositif*: it reveals the ability of the image, through the lens of the spectator's visual perception and investment in the aural narrative, to be seen repeatedly and in turn generate new meanings. Through her repeated showing of the photographs that constitute *Travelogue*, Charlotte Moth also explores the same potential of redundancy, of seeing again, and articulating anew the images that she, or chosen narrators, manipulate.
fig. 6 — In her two films, *Sadie Murdoch* and *Maeve Connolly* (both 2010), Moth invites the theorist Maevc Connelly and the artist Sadie Murdoch to look at a set of images from *Travelogue*. Both films are black and white photo-films, yet their visual sequences function differently: in *Sadie Murdoch*, Sadie is photographed as she looks at the images – the camera moves between her figure and the table where the photographs are laid out – while her comments are recorded and later played as voice-over for the film; in *Maeve Connolly*, the film is made of the photographs themselves with Connolly's comments as voice-over. The repetition and circulation of the gaze produces new relations and multiply the narrative possibilities. *Travelogue* thus appears as 'the space of an infinite work of construction, able to elaborate, through its scaffoldings, its labyrinths and its slopes, the equivalent of a reality forever mute.'[9]

The visual reduction that Marcelline Delbecq operates in her works, which affirms the power of the text and of the reader's voice over the image in the construction of a cinematic experience, immediately echoes the works that Marguerite Duras carried out as a filmmaker in the late 1970s and the early 1980s. In the late 1970s, Duras made two other short films, *Les Mains Négatives* (1979) and *Césarée* (1979). *Les Mains Négatives* uses a long uncut sequence of film recorded by driving through Paris at night until dawn. *Césarée* brings together long travelling sequences of the gardens of the Tuileries near the Louvre, the linear movement of the camera sweeping over Aristide Maillol's immobile bronze sculptures; very still shots of monumental sculptures covered in scaffolding, and blown up shots of the hieroglyphs on the Obélisque erected in the centre of the Place de la Concorde. Both films are made with remainders of filmed sequences from her shooting of the feature-length film *Navire Night* (1978). The text in *Césarée* and *Les Mains Négatives* has little if anything to do with the images, introducing an essential gap and discrepancy between image and narrative. As Duras has stated:

> *I am in a relation of murder with cinema. I started to make films to reach the creative gain of the destruction of the text. Now I want to reach the image, reduce it. I'm considering a universal image ('une image passe-partout') that can infinitely overlap with a series of texts, an image neither beautiful nor ugly that would take on meaning only from the text that passes over it.*(10)

However this 'image passe-partout' is not just any image. Through the process of destruction of the image that Duras deploys in her films, which, as she suggests, shares some commonality with her work with text, she searches for an ideal image, an image isolated from a visual grammar. Her relationship to the image echoes her relationship to words that she describes as existing outside of a grammar of language; words such as: 'sea', 'sun', 'night', 'time', 'transit', 'house', 'table', 'death', 'wind', 'river', 'flat', 'plenitude', 'sand' or 'intensity'.(11) The visual sequences that are used for *Césarée*, *les Mains Négatives*, *Le Camion*, *Aurélia Steiner (Melbourne)* (1979), *Aurélia Steiner (Vancouver)* (1979), and for *l'Homme Atlantique* (1981), focus on the sea or on the river, on the movement of a car through the streets of Paris or of a lorry on the road. These 'natural' movements, rhythmically marking the passing of time, seem to substitute themselves to the mechanical movement of the camera – something we could compare to Hollis Frampton's use of fire in order to insert movement into the texture of his still images:

> *Here the film does not say anything. Its evolution is difficult to apprehend, it does not seem to change, to progress, to move forward, it seems to be mobile only in relation to itself, to an axis of immobility that it would have imposed on itself during its entire journey. Change, real or apparent, is not exterior to the film; the film contains it. Thus this immobility, this axis of fixity around which it revolves, retains it in itself. Nothing leaves, lightens its density.*(12)

References to interior spaces punctuate Duras' films such as *Le Camion*, in which she brings the film into her own working space, or in *l'Homme Atlantique*, in which the text refers to the entrance hall of the hotel Les Roches Noires in Trouville, Normandy. The opposition between interior and exterior indexes the tension between the space of the text and the space of the image, the attempt to communicate and the interiority of the affects. Chaimowicz's fig. 7 __ performance piece *Partial Eclipse...* (1980-2006) stages a somehow similar experience. A series of slides are projected in a dark space, the images describe the interior space of a London apartment – looking through rooms, objects and furniture, and showing a male figure, presumably the artist, within this highly composed living space. The voice-over begins with a woman reading fragments of text that overlay the images, adding words in an attempt to qualify the atmosphere of the space, the mode of existence of the artist and perhaps their relationship. The ambivalence of the object of the narrator's description – the space which mirrors the nature of the relationship of the two protagonists – gives to the voice-over an extremely fluid quality despite its redundancy. There is a sense of stillness that the still photographs unfold sequentially on the screen and the rhythm of the voice, slowly articulating one word after the other, confer on the film-like slide sequence. The voice of a male character, the artist himself, takes over halfway through the film, and yet his presence was already twice embodied through his image within the photographs, and through his enigmatic wandering within the space, passing through the projection, becoming the screen and inserting himself into the images in the actuality of his physical presence.(13) Layers of different temporalities accumulate, and the two narrators continuously remind the spectators of the ambiguity of the scenes they are looking at. *Partial Eclipse...* materialises the space of physical and emotional intimacy through the invention of the spatial configuration of the performance and film, shifting the perception of lived experience into the field of a constructed fiction. The performance never stops moving between actuality – of memory, of presence – and fantasy. 'The separation between real and fictive is obscured but accessible', says the male narrator in the film. The distinction between identified persons and fictional characters has also become blurred. The voices of the two narrators never converse; the shared intimacy, the opening up of the interior living space to the presence of the other, belongs to the past. The gaps between past and present, and between two subjective experiences, become visible in the intense fragmentation of the work, its collage of solitary voices, images and drifting presence. And yet the voices and the embodied male presence address a common virtual space, the space of the film. The film holds an indifferent plasticity and appears infinitely malleable by the voices that qualify the images and the experience that they witness. As Janet Harbord has remarked about Chris Marker's *La Jetée* (1962), the images: 'belong neither to a time nor a place, but to a way of imagining and making the world as a scene, a range of different textures, memories and fantasies that resist temporal classification.'(14) This affinity between such collaged sequences of images and the experience of writing is of seminal importance in Chaimowicz's work. The essential activity of reading generates visual as well as written work, influenced by writers such as Marguerite Duras, Jean Cocteau or Jean Genet.

Le Parc (1984) is a text by Chaimowicz that is accompanied by scattered images such as a large boat and an industrial harbour, or a sign spelling the word 'voyage' in art deco style. The text weaves together the thoughts of two characters, a man and a woman: 'I recently dreamed that we shared the same thoughts, that I echoed your sentiments.' These words open the two-voice narrative. The characters have no particular names, Chaimowicz may call them 'he' and 'she' for convenience. The text creates a space of writing densely filled with sophisticated descriptions of the surroundings that punctuate the narrative with intense visual moments:

> *Gradually I deciphered a foreground that was of sand... a beach merging into sea and then sky... Drawn to this unlikely image, I wished to enter its picture frame, and so, with trepidation, stepped out onto a balcony... An arc of deserted beach startled me. It was as though a forgotten and exotic postcard had slipped from the pages of a long discarded book...*(15)

Here the flow of words mirrors a very peculiar sense of time, proper to the rhythm of thoughts and reverie. During our conversation about *Le Parc*, Chaimowicz recalled the short novel that Marguerite Duras had published in 1955, *Le Square*. Duras said that she wrote it by listening to people being quiet in the small public gardens of Paris:

> *She, she finds herself there every afternoon, alone most of the time in the apparent daze of pure rest. She, she looks after the children of someone else. He is barely a salesman that sells on markets these small objects that one so often forgets to buy. They are both looking at time folding and unfolding.*(16)

Thus in homage to Duras, and perhaps to Jean Genet who famously enjoyed the brutal atmosphere of industrial harbours, Chaimowicz set up his own narrative in a provincial city close to the sea, whose own tranquillity seems to guide the pace of the story. *Le Parc* is therefore a text that was written for two voices and can be staged as a public reading, accompanied by black and white slides, including the text itself. In a manner similar to *Partial Eclipse...*, the two voices are not formally in dialogue. Half-way through the narrative, which appears to recount a trip that the two characters, perhaps a couple, had shared, a park is described; but as the park emerges, it reveals more strongly the ambiguous temporality of the narrative, moving both characters into the interiority of their thoughts and their memory. He and she seem to converge into the two facets of one being; the distance between them reduces to the point of confusion. What seemed at first to be the story of a relationship gradually shifts towards the parallel movement of two solitary paths. The circulation of the voices in the performance incorporates this fluidity, and the embodiment of the characters in these two distinct reading voices that do not directly address each other anchor the narrative in a fragmented literary experience.

The coexistence of male and female voices implies a relationship, and more precisely a relationship where love and desire are central. Both *Le Parc* and *Partial Eclipse...* stage the sharing of cinematic space between two autonomous voices that do not directly address each other; it's a 'silent dialogue' or the echoing of shared thoughts. With *Césarée*, Marguerite Duras begins to limit the use of the voice to her own, something she will pursue in *Les Mains Négatives*, *Aurélia Steiner*, and *l'Homme Atlantique*. There are no longer traditional characters but only the voice of a unique author/narrator/character:

> *So the voice is transformed into an appeal, a speech act, in the same moment as need is transformed into desire; it is caught in a drama of appeal, eliciting an answer, provocation, demand, love.*(17)

Duras' disembodied voice directly addresses absence and lack, and this voice of unknown origins creates an audible space that unfolds a dramatic tension, in contrast with the ghostly landscapes that slowly move across the screen. The identity of the voice remains enigmatic, the voice-over is diverted from its traditional function: neither objective voice of the commentator nor subjective voice of the narrator; it fluctuates between multiple identities, as it also constantly shifts the identity of the addressee. The voice is the voice of a text, whose traditional narrative structure has itself been profoundly transformed through Duras' writing. Through the use of her voice, Duras attempts to intervene as little as possible, emptying her reading of any dramatic intonation that would impose emotions and thus over-determine meaning. She writes:

> *Meaning will come after, it does not need me. The voice of reading alone will give it without my intervention. Reading is proposed out loud in the same way as it is proposed for you alone, the first time, without voice. This slowness, this lack of discipline of punctuation is as if I was undressing the words, one after the other, and that I discovered what was underneath, the isolated word, unrecognisable, deprived of any relationship, of any identity, abandoned... We perceive that when we say, when we listen, how much words are friable and can crumble into dust.*(18)

And yet the voice in Duras' films acquires a particular dimension as she comes to privilege sound over images in her approach to cinema. The voice produces the film, leads its narrative and invokes images that she puts in tension with the film's moving images. As Mladen Dolar notes about the use of the voice in the birth of the Opera: '...the dramatic tension between the word and the voice was put into its cradle, and their impossible and problematic relationship presented its driving force.'(19) And if Duras' voice finds itself at the opposite spectrum of the Opera's singing voice, it nevertheless comes to play a central role. Duras' discourse seems to demonstrate that she considers the voice as secondary to the text, as a remainder on the edge of the literary experience. Dolar stresses that this reduction of the voice, the ambivalence of its position within the linguistic operation that 'produces the voice as the object.'(20) One might add:

an object of desire, the disembodied manifestation of a presence. In Duras' work, voice and text are invested with a unique sense of materiality, of reality, that images cannot achieve... until Duras decides to entirely annihilate the visual by proposing a black image in *L'Homme Atlantique*: 'With the black film, I might thus have arrived at an ideal image, the one of the confessed murder of cinema.'[21]

> *Sitting at a table in a deserted Billancourt studio, she proposed a version of the film which nobody else could possibly have thought of: Duras, alone, in a white polo-neck sweater and wearing tortoise-shell glasses, her novel in her hand, only reads those parts of L'Amant that she feels like reading, and strays outside of the text with a delightful naturalness. Her voice can be recognised out of thousands – turn by turn that of the young girl, of the woman eaten away by life, of the author, of the heroine, of the present and of memory, real or phantasmagorical. Her long-lasting reading makes it obvious that if L'Amant was to become a film, it would require neither actor nor actress, still less of sets and extras. Her voice is the film, the one that enables her to plunge, and plunge again, and go astray in her own book.*[22]

Like Duras, Delbecq has been exploring through her work the potential for the voice to produce visually acoustic sensations. Her long-lasting interest in photography and cinema has imprinted in her memory an infinite number of dispersed visual and auditory fragments that form an 'erratic slide show'.[23] The artist has gradually engaged with writing and storytelling to bring her infinite cinema to life, willingly choosing the narrating voice as her preferred mode of operation when it comes to animate her combinations of text and images. Female voices have been the central protagonists of this artistic construction. Kim Gordon, the mythical singer of the music band *Sonic Youth*, gave her voice to the text of *Rapture*, elected by Delbecq to coalesce a sense of generational collective memory and the evocation of her own personal youth. It is nevertheless the voice of the actress Elina Löwensohn that has durably given a timbre and a rhythm to Delbecq's narratives:

> *Through a voice that is no longer quite hers, or quite another, she accepted the delicate mission to embody a succession of appearances and disappearances, to which the listener's imagination alone can give a form.*[24]

Alternately narrator or anonymous character, Elina's voice is for Delbecq one of these fragments that beats time in her own history of cinema. And yet Delbecq has also used her own voice in her works, following in the path of Duras, letting her gentle voice bring to presence some of her elusive fictional figures and haunt the mind of her listeners with many mysterious scenarios.

> *A polymorphous camera has always turned, and will turn forever, its lens focused upon all the appearances of the world. Before the invention of still photography, the frames of the infinite cinema were blank, black leader; then a few images began to appear upon the endless ribbon of film. Since the birth of photographic cinema, all the frames are filled with images.*[25]

Frampton and Duras have convoked the black image in their films, referring to black leader not to evoke a time prior to cinema but to explore new possibilities for filmmaking. Disfiguring the traditional cinematic apparatus to question again the relations between sound and images, voices and bodies, stillness and movement, has been central to artists who consider filmmaking as an essentially heterogeneous practice, rich of radically different possibilities, and within which the notions of performance and narration can constantly be defined anew.

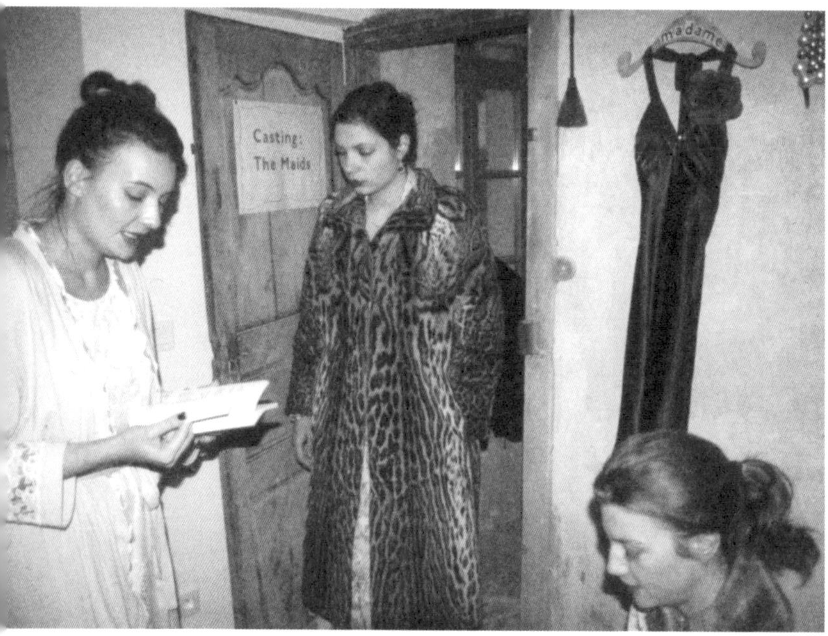

Marc Camille Chaimowicz, *The Casting of the Maids* (2011): documentation during filming. Photo: Marc Camille Chaimowicz.

ENDNOTES

(1) Original quote: 'Les tirages reproduisent sans le savoir des images qui appartiennent depuis longtemps à l'Histoire et ne font que se répéter; l'apparition du grain sur le papier tient inlassablement du miracle, encore et toujours capable de piéger les couples meurtriers dans leur fuite.' *Trafic 72*, December 2009, P.O.L. (Author's translation).

(2) Rachel Moore, *Hollis Frampton (nostalgia)* (London: Afterall Books, 2006), p. 1.

(3) *Ibid.*

(4) Caroline Hancock, 'Poetics of space à la Moth of St Ouen', *Catalogue* magazine, issue 4, http://www.cataloguemagazine.com/contemporary-art/magazine/article/charlotte-moth/

(5) *Ibid.*

(6) 'An Evening with Hollis Frampton', 8 March 1973. Sound Recordings of Museum-Related Events, 70.22. The Museum of Modern Art Archives, New York. Quoted by Rachel Moore in *Hollis Frampton (nostalgia)* (London: Afterall Books, 2006), p. 5.

(7) Mladen Dolar, *A voice and nothing more* (Cambridge, Massachusetts: MIT Press, 2006), p. 79.

(8) Jacques Rancière, *La fable cinématographique* (Paris: Seuil, 2001), pp. 145 (Author's translation)

(9) Jacques Rancière, *La fable cinématographique* (Seuil, Paris, 2001), p. 205 (Author's translation)

(10) Marguerite Duras, 'Les Yeux Verts', *Les Cahiers du cinéma*, 312-313, June 1980 p. 49 (Author's translation).

(11) See Marguerite Duras, *Work and Words* (1984): video, duration: 57 minutes, colour.

(12) Marguerite Duras, 'Les Yeux Verts', *Les Cahiers du cinéma*, 312-313, June 1980 (my translation).

(13) Since 2006, Marc Camille Chaimowicz has used surrogates to embody himself in the performance, choosing men sharing resemblance with him at the time of the photographs. *Partial Eclipse...* (1980-2006) has been performed most recently at Tate Britain in the context of the museum's temporary collection displays *Has the Film Already Started?* (27 June 2011 - 26 February 2012).

(14) Janet Harbord, *Chris Marker La Jetée* (London: Afterall Books, 2009), p. 25.

(15) Marc Camille Chaimowicz, *Le Parc, An Illustrated Text for Two Voices*, 1984.

(16) Marguerite Duras in *L'Express*, 14th September 1956 (Author's translation).

(17) Mladen Dolar, *A voice and nothing more* (Cambridge, Massachusetts: MIT Press, 2006), p. 28.

(18) Marguerite Duras, 'Les Yeux Verts', *Les Cahiers du cinéma*, 312-313, June 1980, pp. 49 (my translation).

(19) Mladen Dolar, *A voice and nothing more*, p. 30.

(20) *Ibid*, p. 36.

(21) Marguerite Duras, 'Les Yeux Verts', *Les Cahiers du cinéma*, 312-313, June 1980, p. 49 (my translation).

(22) Marcelline Delbecq, *Repertory, Volume n°2*, 2011, p. 47.

(23) Marcelline Delbecq, *Des impressions, des ombres, Trafic 72*, December 2009, P.O.L. (Author's translation).

(24) *Ibid.*

(25) Hollis Frampton, 'For a Metahistory of Film', *Circles of Confusion* (Rochester: Visual Studies Workshop Press, 1983), p. 111: in Rachel Moore, *Hollis Frampton (nostalgia)*, p. 51.

I wish to thank Jack Needell and Becky Weston, students on the BA filmmaking at Kingston University, who recorded and transcribed the original extended discussion I had with Clare Gasson, on 9 December 2011 at Goldsmiths, University of London.

Working Songs: 'yes to the connection between voice and audience'

ANNE-SOPHIE DINANT

In the absence of narratives most usually translated through movement and expression, Clare Gasson's live performances and films present *liveness* derived from sound and voice compositions; the voice is thus employed as an immediate source and principal element. Through the act of vocalising texts and scripts written by the artist, both performance and film are linked. In her film work especially, the stage – one of the main elements of theatricality – disappears. And so, in the film *7'* (2010), Gasson becomes an enigmatic personage, a shadow, a silhouetted presence in the video image, a presence that shows us buildings and places in relation to memories while the artist's voice tells us their story (1). Through its mise-en-scène, the film becomes a form of theatre where a narrative unfolds. Gasson's camera slowly scrutinizes photographs – representations of places associated to some other psychological dimension – in a psycho-geographic zone where vestiges of memory are explored. The story is not directly linked to the images or vice versa but, instead, it offers an ambiguity and another place where story and visual presentation link performance and moving image. This connects or channels directly into the viewer's own memories. Working with text and script, Gasson's films are elegantly created through the exploration of sound, juxtaposing it with filmic material in a way whereby the two interact in a very delicate, poetic assemblage. She deliberately uses a *slow* camera or a single take to record her performances, which are produced by her voice and subtle, balanced, simple actions.

The live presentation of works such as *The River* (2011) and *The Traveller Walking Walking Walking Through* (2010) transports the viewer in a performative yet cinematic way. (2) In *The Traveller* fig. 8 — *Walking Walking Walking Through* (2010), Gasson orchestrated a walk through Bath responding to her own experience of a ballad, creating a sound-poem that she presented on stage, played out according to the rhythm of waulking songs. And *The River*, composed in collaboration with musicologist Huw Hallam, consists of a multi-layered text piece, sung by a group of musicians and vocalists. Presented on a small, transportable stage that is placed centrally, the temporary stage allows the audience to move freely around it, perceiving different intonations of the voices as they disperse frequencies emanating from a central source (the stage). Eight vocalists read out name-lists, which are intoned impressively with the waves of their voices.

IMAGE AND VOICE (FILM AND PERFORMANCE)

Gasson's work forms a particularly engaging relationship between film and performance where image and sound coincide through the pre-eminence or abiding centrality of the *voice*. It is as if the image goes with the *flow* of the voice, the voice itself taking on a pivotal, aural significance.

At the moment I am interested in not editing the image at all – the sound though is highly worked. There is a performative element about using one take – lots of chance coming in. There is a very simple internal structure. It's not slap-dash however – a lot of planning goes into it. The sound is created separately – and is its own world – hovering and detached from the image. The sound is often recorded in advance, but when we put sound and image together a lot of unexpected connections occur. I don't, for example, want everything synced in a very constructed, obvious way – although of course sometimes this happens unexpectedly.

In everything I do the audience is very important. I want them to feel the pieces and be immersed in the film or performance – to really feel the work, as there is a visceral quality in everything I do and make. I suppose this is the case for The River *– to create a happening, a whole piece where everyone is implicated and touched by it somehow. Film and the filmic process are referenced in most of my work but in the script rather than literally filming something. In this way the sound pieces can literally be shown as films – screened in cinema spaces as films in sound, using the structure of cinema to have the audience in a physical, cinematic space.*(3)

MATERIALITY OF THE VOICE

The list of names used as material for *The River* was compiled during Gasson's exploration of the archive at the Women's Art Library (WAL), housed at Goldsmiths, University of London. Although her initial idea was to create a work around the manifestos written by women artists and held in the archive, she instead decided on using an inventory of all the names appearing in the Library's catalogues. Her emphasis therefore shifted from researching pre-existing manifestos to the presentation of every archived name as an enumeration of memory, a live *memorial* to the artists represented in the library. Clare spent six months at WAL developing this piece, and *The River* is in a sense also a type of manifesto – an indexical vocalisation of all contributing names.

Created at the end of the 1970s, WAL provided a platform for women artists to show their work to a broader audience. The collection of exhibition catalogues covers women's art from the 70s. It was a place in which to bring together information on particular artists but equally a centre for feminist activity. Instead of looking through the archive, selecting from its contents, Gasson decided to develop the role of all its previous contributors, bringing them into action again so that the archive itself emerges through her work as a new directory of names – leading to the creation of a manifesto – that is ultimately transmitted through voice as a material form.

INTRODUCING THE IDEA OF LABOUR – MAKING THE VOICE (STARTING WITH MAKING POSTERS, TRANSPOSED TO THE VOICE)

Also connected to *The River* is a series of posters which Gasson has created using a mixture of articles, newspaper clippings, photographs form the WAL archive and various other sources which mirror the newsletters discovered in the archive. This action of production not only mirrors the form of material found in the archive but acts to introduce the action of labour – manual labour – into the work in a manner connected to the process of walking and *waulking* found in *The Traveller*.

Working with the archive has been really very different to how I usually proceed. The early women's newsletter was literally a cut and paste process: they didn't have computers so they typed everything on a typewriter, cutting and pasting it on an A3 sheet and then photocopying it; that was how it was made. Additionally, I live and work in a place that is something of an archive as well, in a way. The posters I made for the exhibition used articles and flyers from shows, press releases from shows, as well as photocopies from old and worn newspapers from the Women's Art Library. Many of the quotes used on the posters have been around me forever, although some of them are from manifestos...

Making posters, writing scripts for songs, song-poems, using laborious processes for text and so on introduces the double notion of manual labour and the body at work, producing the body's voice. What the repetition of work and voice brings together is the basic recipe for the creation of certain beat-driven song forms, such as workers songs and more specifically, waulking songs – songs that were created specifically in order to assist the processes (rhythm, motion) of labour. For *The River*, Gasson worked with professional singers, working with them, creating rhythms emanating from the script so that labour is directly connected to the physical work of the body through the voice.

The absolute strictness of working with lists is very interesting to me because it has a repetitive labour element to it; assembling something governed by the beat, corresponding to something you're actually doing with material, whether it's writing or typing. I wanted to get to a point where the vocalists could actually all split rhythms across a name, but that's quite difficult when they are going at different rhythms. I see it as a piece that can continue to grow in complexity and be reworked.

The intention is to extend this process, directly connecting it performatively to the viewer, as is communicated by one of the sentences inscribed on the poster accompanying the exhibition:

Yes to the connection between the voice and the audience.

SCULPTURES AS METAPHOR FOR THE VOICE

fig. 9 — Gasson produced several sculptures for the exhibition at WAL. It appears as if they are placed as metaphors for the making of an artwork, taking the form of concrete objects, whilst introducing direct connections with performance. They are representations of the performers but they might indirectly also stand as a personification of elements from the archive.

There's a definite link between the performances and the sculptures, the framed pieces, the posters and photographs. They all look to performance, the live act, film and theatre. The sculptures are made of self-drying clay. I decided that I wanted them raw, as it seemed to go well with the idea of manifestos. The sculptures work in a different way. When I was producing the score, I was at the computer going through a file: approximately 41 pages of names. It was intense. So making the sculpture introduced a very different manner of thinking. The idea was to make these clay things that were characters and held the essence of the text. So the ones at WAL and

SLG [South London Gallery] were like 'manifesto performers'. I was thinking about the various manifestos when I was making them, trying to get the movement. In that way, a manifesto isn't so much an organic thing, but these names are. They are part of a very historical whole.

STAGING THE VOICE (MAKING OF RHYTHM)

The relation between stage and rhythm in Gasson's live performances appears as a way to underline the theatricality of the piece. Even when the stage is not actually in the film – a sort of invisible stage remains, abstractly rendered through different elements.

That's what I loved about getting on the stage at Arnolfini. I had a pre-recorded text-track which became almost like a metronome, and then I had live clapping and clicking, which was supposed to be fluid. I was sitting on a wooden box that was miked-up, which I also used as a drum to keep the beat. Often, at points, I was in sync with the pre-recorded voice, but I also went out of sync and it became quite improvisational. It all became about timing, because I had to hit quite a few beats along the way to almost underline what was being said. The performance becomes enveloped in timing.

MAKING OF THE VOICE AS SOCIAL EXPERIENCE

In *The River*, as in *The Traveller Walking Walking Walking Through*, there is this same desire for the rhythm creation being the heart of the work, reiterating the tradition and social significance of the waulking song. These beat-driven Scottish folk songs were used by women to accompany the act of waulking cloth.(4) Created to be sung in groups, to be paired with working, they intrinsically bear a social form.

The women waulking the cloth would sing. Then there would be a call and response and they would make up verses and have a refrain within the songs. You start to realise that working songs like miner's songs or sea shanties throughout time have often emerged from the boringness or monotony of labour. There is a huge archive of these songs. The Blues, for example, has come out of that. Almost everything comes with a rhythm for me; when you're writing it comes with a rhythm and trips over into singing regularly, even if it's not obvious. I'm often writing ballads or listening to the musicality within the text as a clue to whether it works or not. In ballads, rhythm is very important because they look to social history and are political in many ways. They can be as neat and short and succinct and as powerful as a poem.

TEXT AND VOICE

The relationship between text and musicality is very present in Gasson's work, becoming the base and the intrinsic materiality of the text; this texture is the primary material for making the work. There is therefore a strong sense of using voice as object-making. The voice becomes this raw material, the texture for the making of a live work. It can be compared to the malleable material used to make a sculpture. The work on the voice is often performed with a group of people, bringing different steps in the process of making the voice.

Once we tripped into singing and everybody was using the texture of their own voice, I wanted a whole range of voices and it was really important to have men in The River *along with different tonal ranges so that the texture was as rich as possible between male and female. Some women can be falsetto (it's not all soprano) and the same with men, their voices can be quite high or low. So once they started to push into the musicality of it, we got these beautiful tones; that's what I mean when I talk about texture.*

In Gasson's films, there is an absence of traditional narratives. Narrative-structure is conveyed through movements and expression, and liveness comes from sound and voice. The stage, one of the main elements of theatricality, disappears in Gasson's work and the filmic image itself becomes the theatre of a story. Camera movements scrutinize objects or photographs, representations of places associated to some other psychological dimension, where vestiges of memory are explored. Therefore another space expands, situated between performance and still image and, as in *The River* or in *The Traveller Walking Walking Walking Through*, both performed on the stage, the viewer is transported through the musicality of the voice.

ENDNOTES

(1) Clare Gasson's video, *7'* (2010) was commissioned by LUX for their project, *Thinking Through Cinema (Deep Red)*, at the Artissima Art Fair in Turin.

(2) As the recipient of The Women's Art Library/Make and Feminist Review research bursary 2011, Clare Gasson presented an exhibition at the Women's Art Library, Goldsmiths, University of London and a live performance at the South London Gallery (SLG), in November 2011. *The Traveller Walking Walking Walking Through* (2010) was commissioned by Bridget Crone / Media Art Bath. It was first performed at Arnolfini, Bristol (June 2010) and subsequently on-site in Bath (August 2010).

(3) All subsequent transcriptions are taken from a conversation with Clare Gasson, 9 December 2011 at Goldsmiths, University of London.

(4) Waulking is a step in Scottish cloth-making that involves the cleansing of cloth to make it thicker. This work was in practice until the 1950s.

Clare Gasson, posters from *The River* (2011): posters made during the Women's Art Library bursary April — Nov 2011. Photo: Asif Din.

"... is the Past
... ve is the Future.
THE velocity of velocities arrives in starting."

M.L. 1914

"... there remains to civic minded, responsible, thrill-seeking females only to overthrow the government, eliminate the money system, institute complete automation ..." V.S. 1967

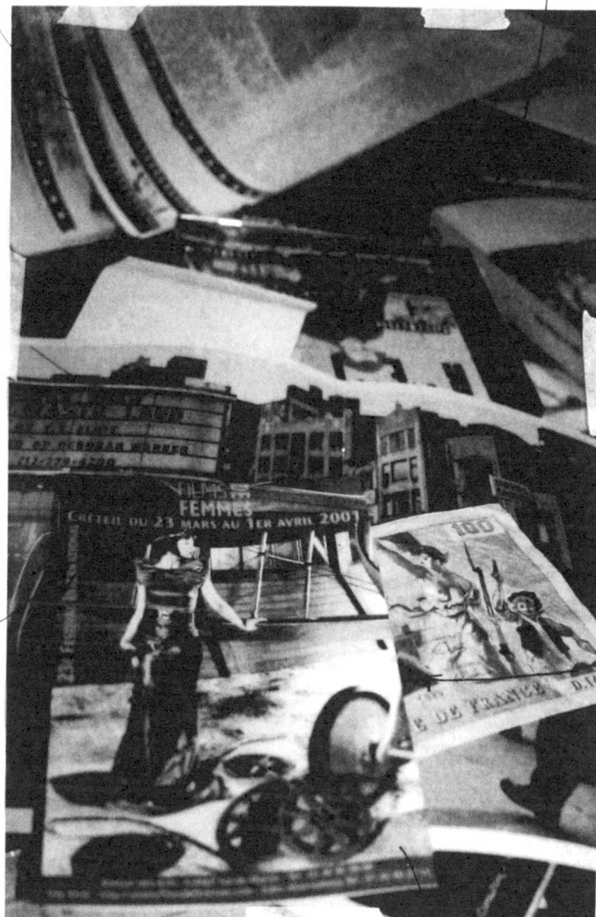

'ART AND WAR ARE THE GREAT MANIFESTATIONS OF SENSUALITY; LUST IS THEIR FLOWER. A people exclusively spiritual or a people exclusively carnal would be condemned to the same decadence - sterility. LUST EXCITES ENERGY AND RELEASES STRENGTH.'

V. de S-P 1913

'... We propose liberating painting from its subservience to the ready-made forms of reality and to make it first and foremost a creative, not a reproductive act.'

O.R 1917

'Humanity is mediocre.
The majority of women are neither superior nor inferior to the majority of men.
They are all equal.
They all merit the same scorn'

V. de S-P 1912 (response to Marinetti)

'LUST IS FORCE'

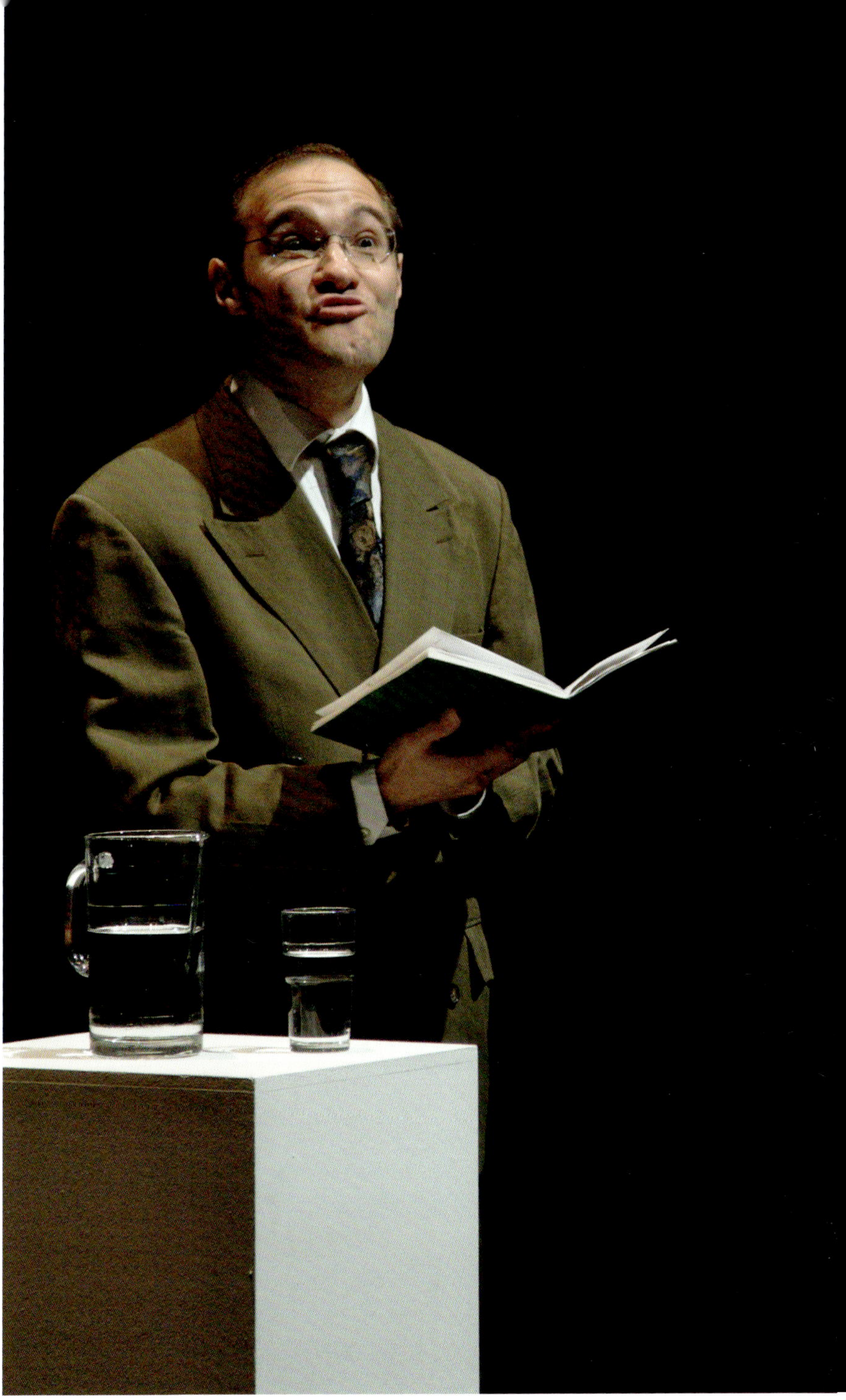

fig. 1 Annabel Frearson, *Frankenstein 2* (2010): performance documentation, part of *A Theatre to Address*, at Arnolfini, Bristol. Photo: Sam Nightingale.

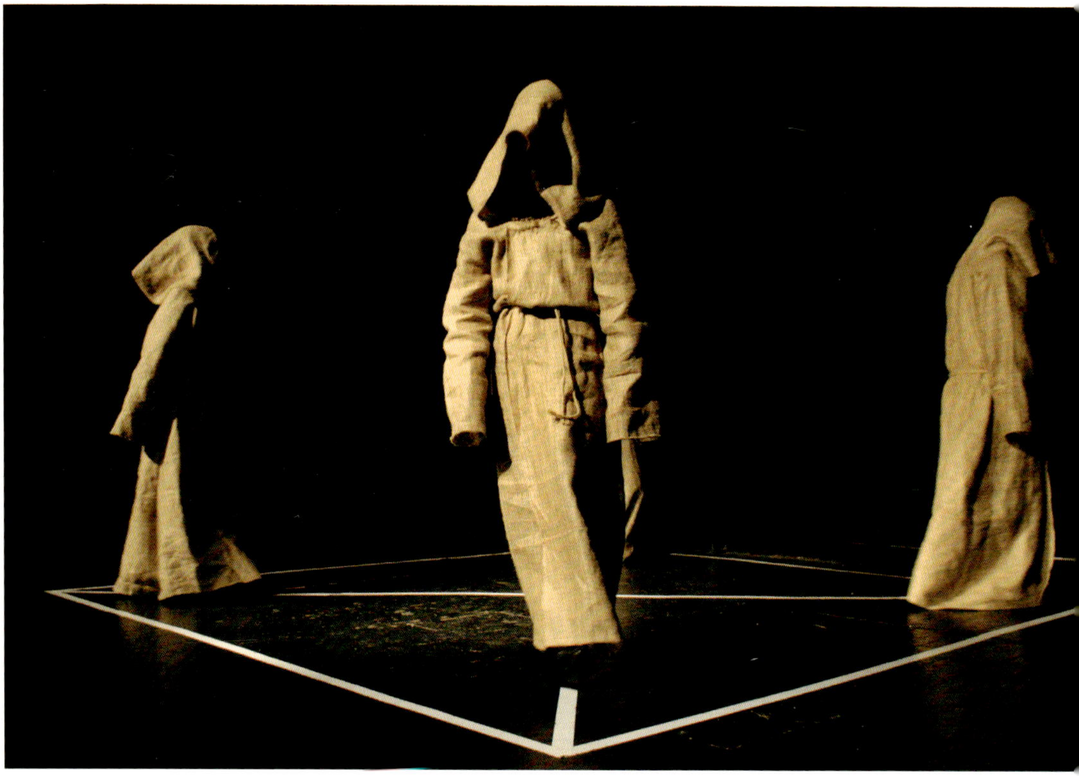

fig. 2 Pil and Galia Kollectiv, *Better Future, Quad-Shaped* (2007): performance documentation, part of *The Sensible Stage*, Cube Microplex, Bristol. Photo: Sam Nightingale.

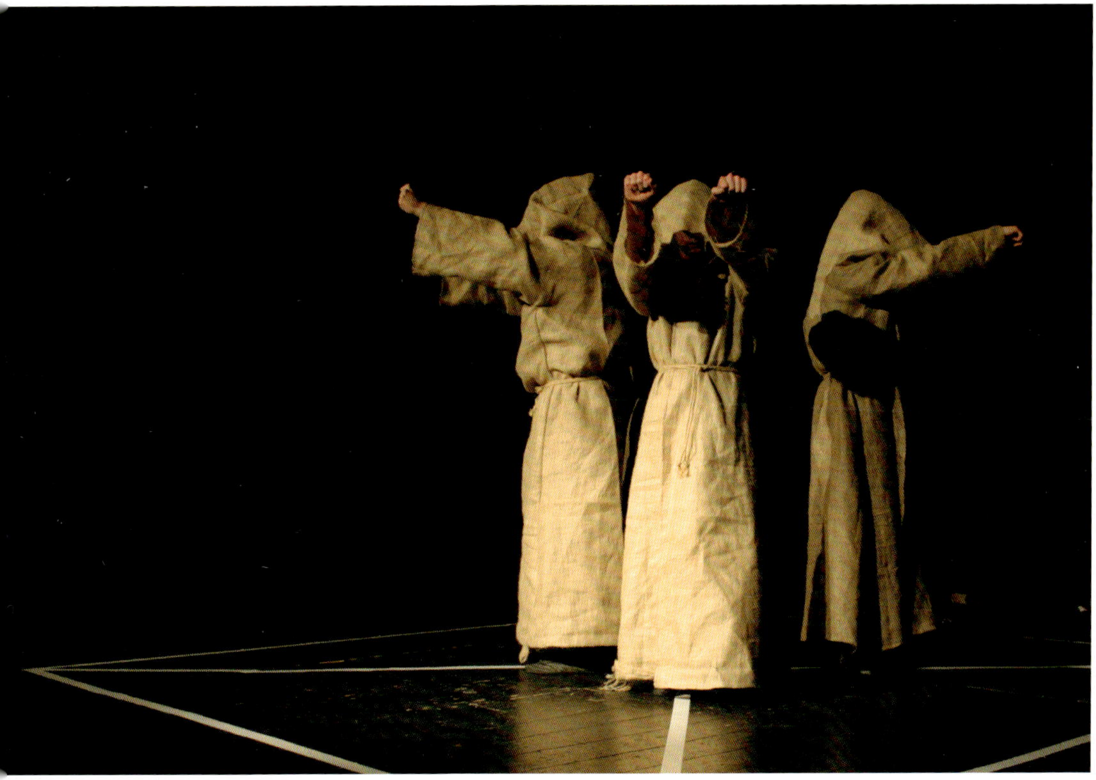

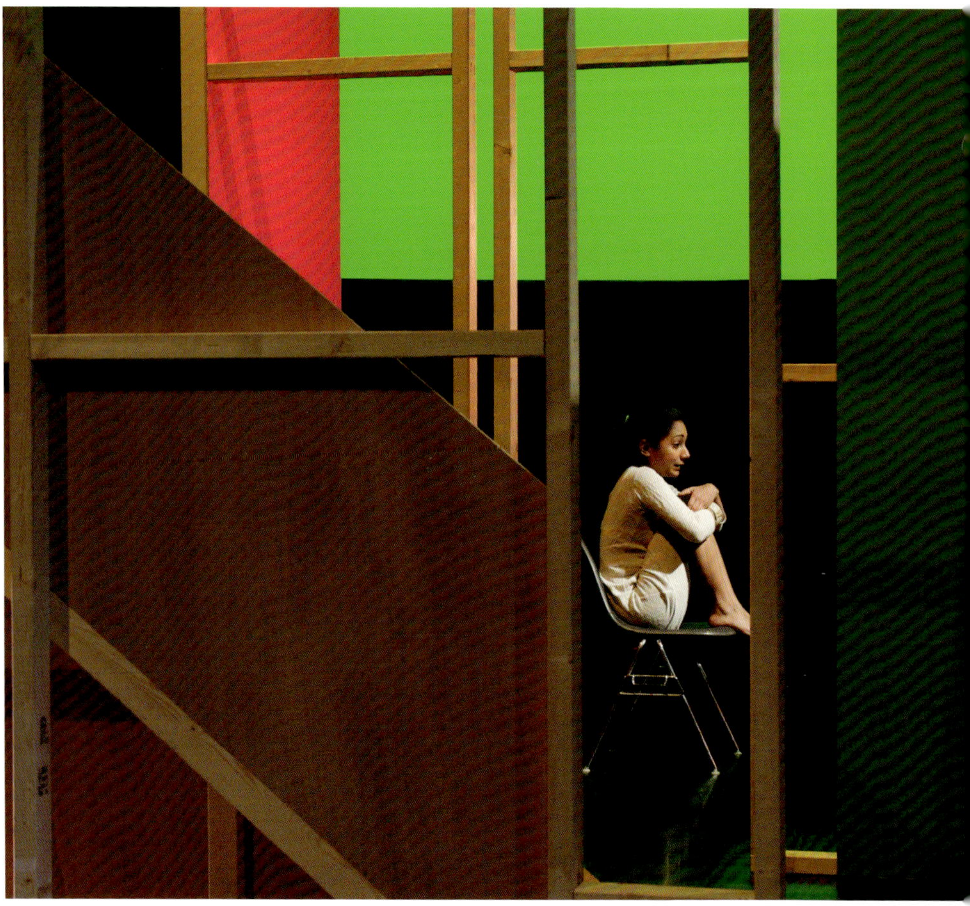

fig. 3 Gail Pickering, *Brutalist Premolition* (2008): performance documentation, Arnolfini, Bristol. Commissioned by Media Art Bath. Photo: Sam Nightingale.

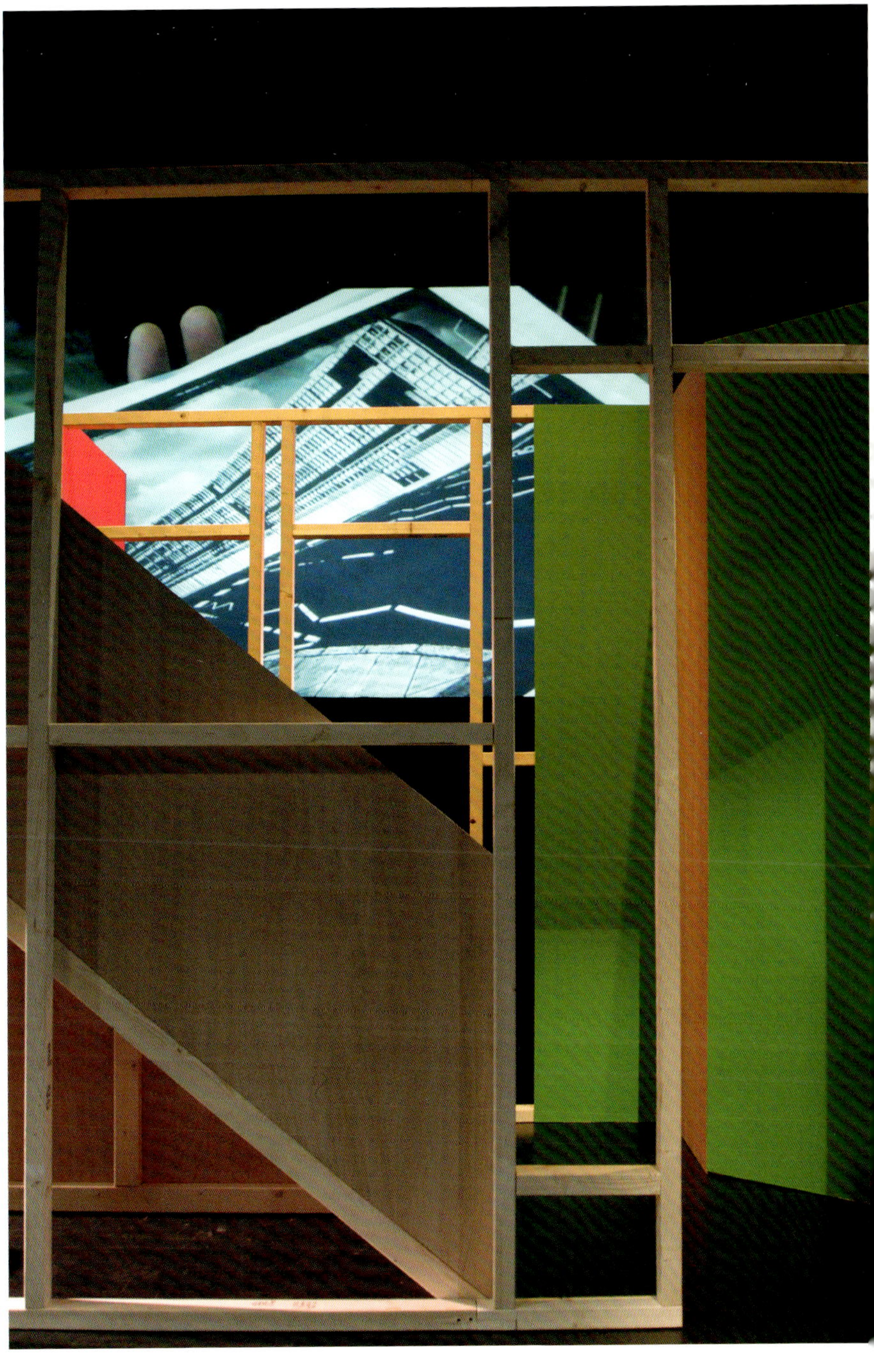

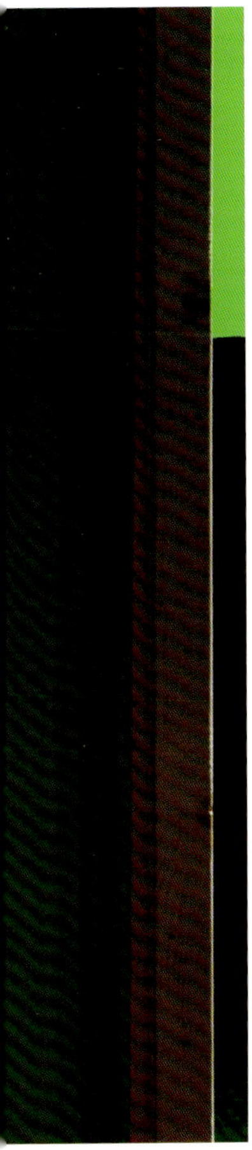

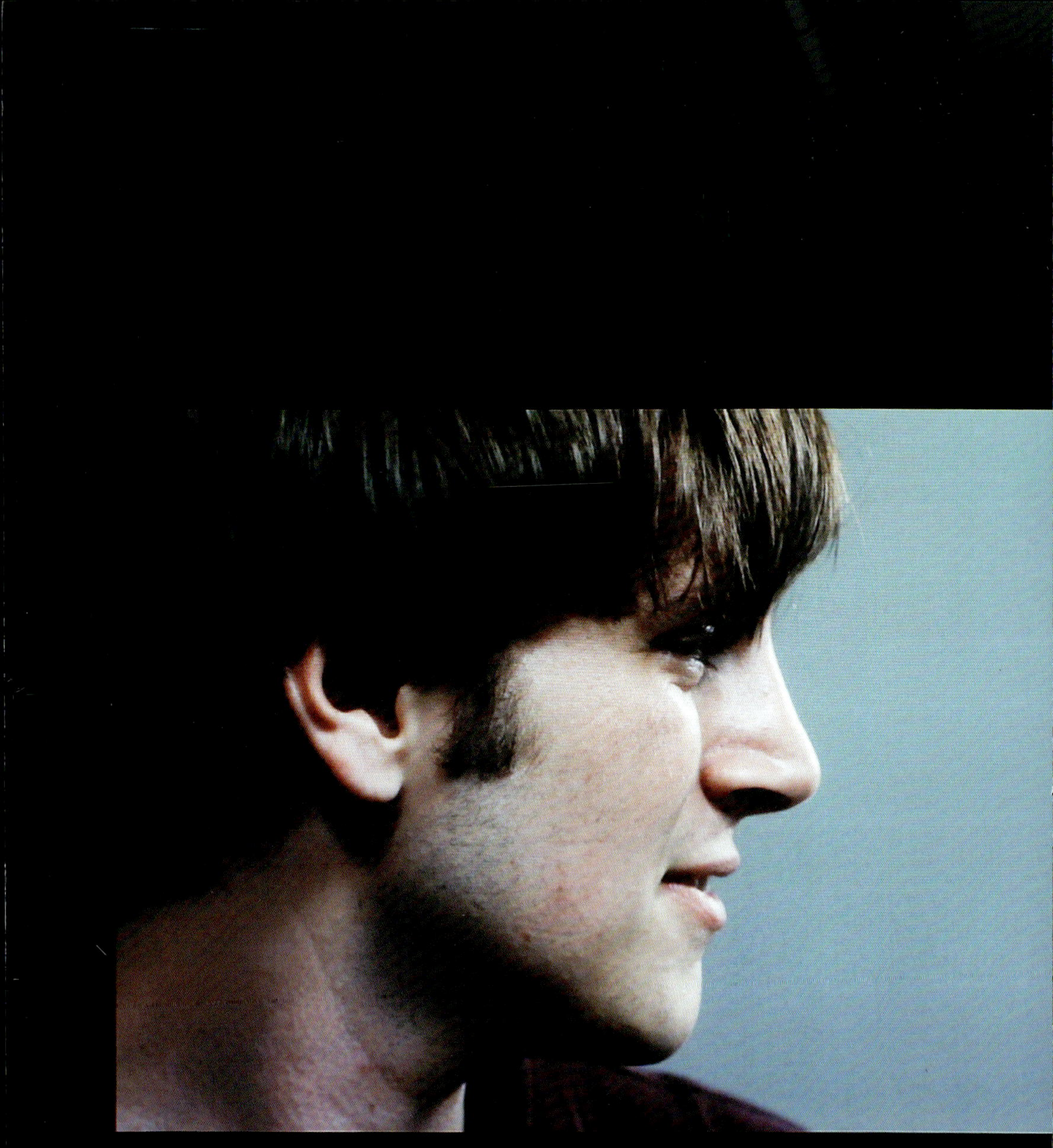

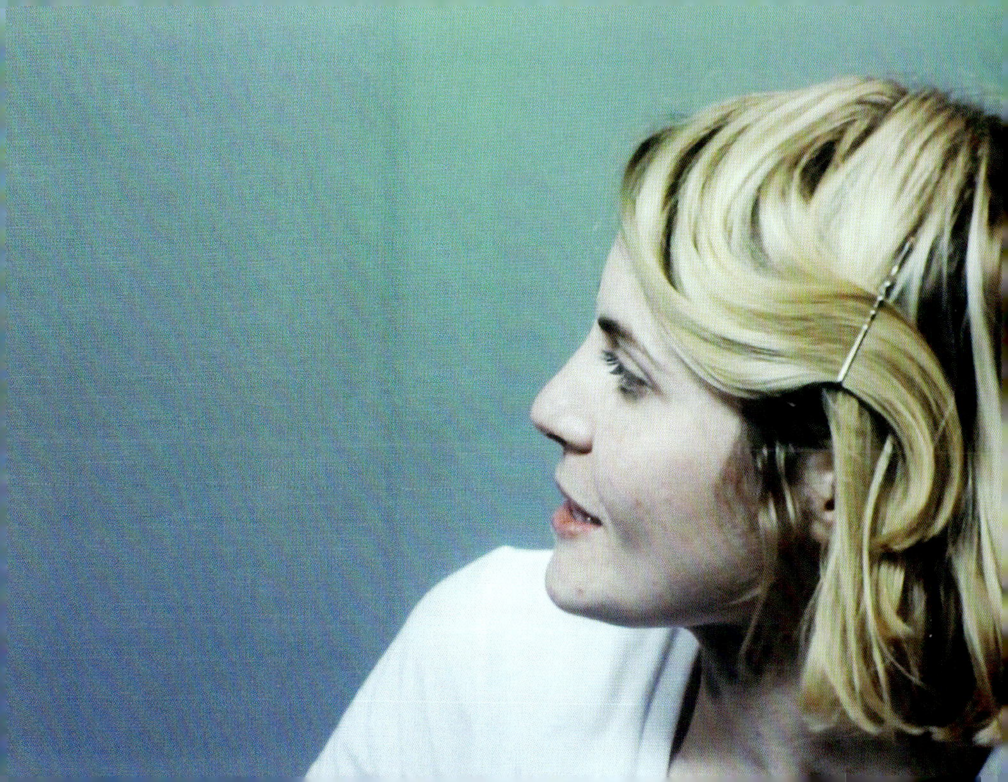

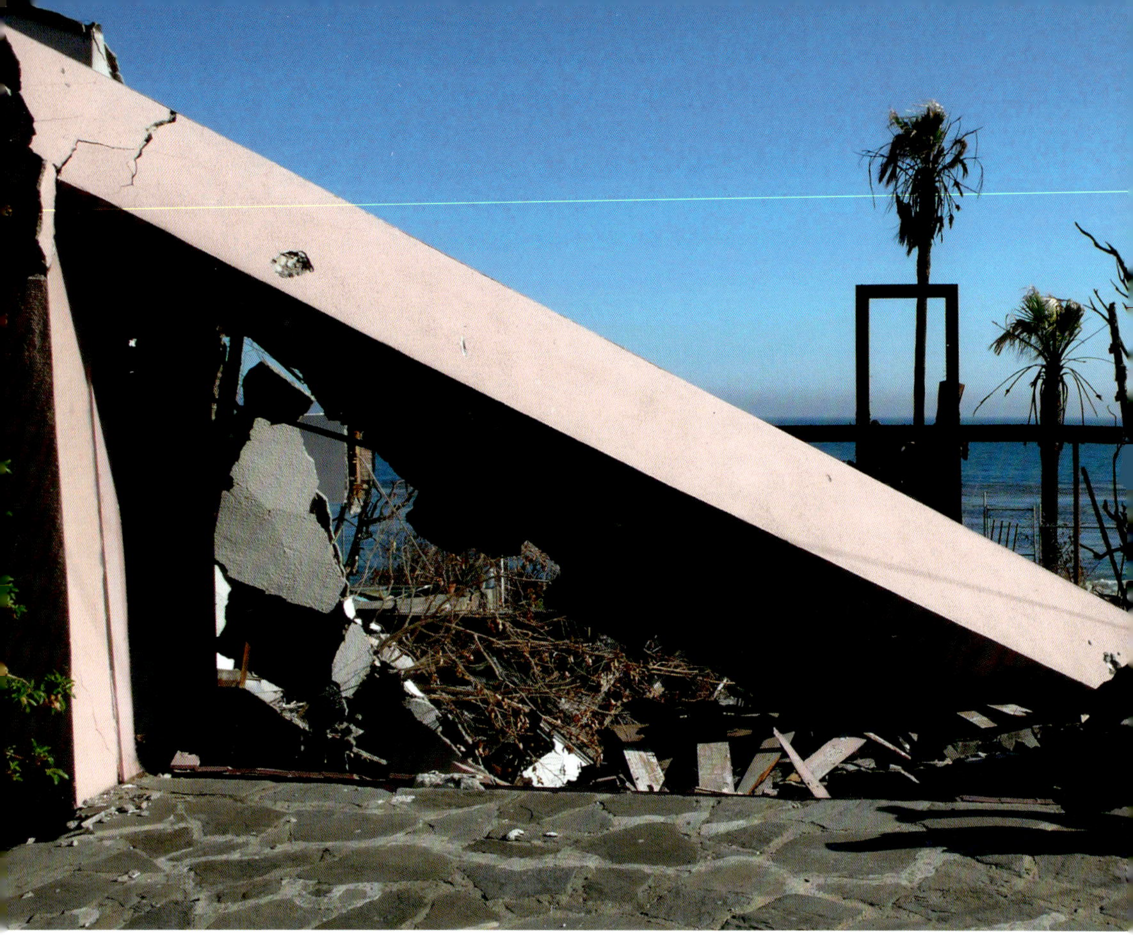

fig. 5 (above) Marcelline Delbecq, *Rapture* (2007): photograph and lightbox.

fig. 6 (right) Charlotte Moth, *Sadie Murdoch* (2010): film still.
Collection FRAC Centre, Orléans / Courtesy Marcelle Alix, Paris.

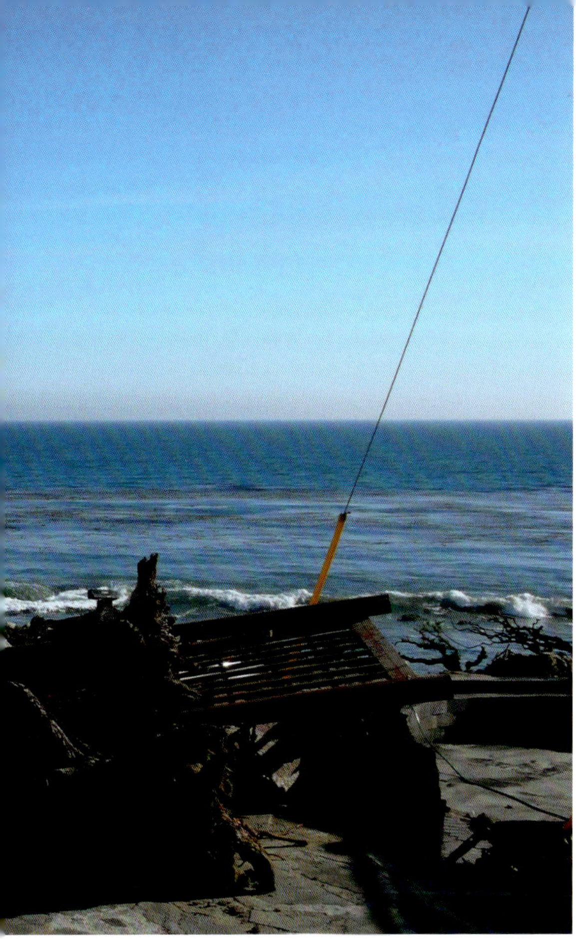

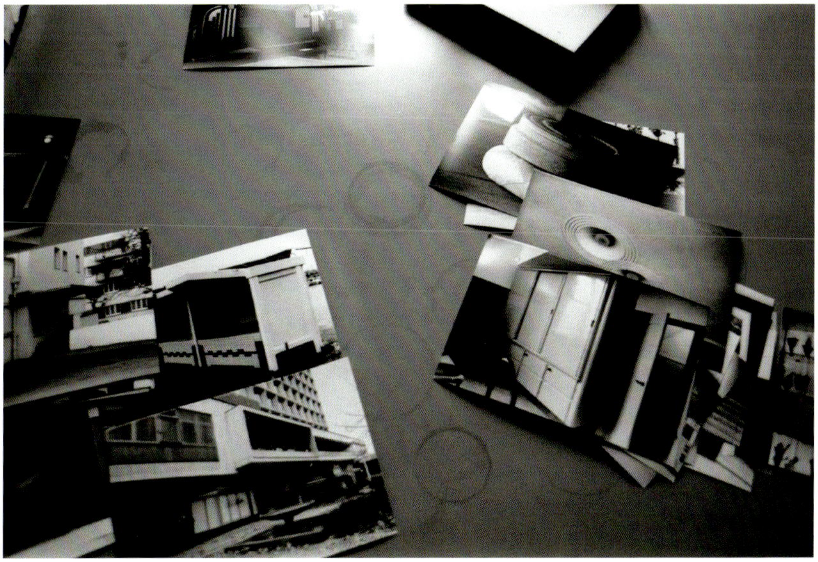

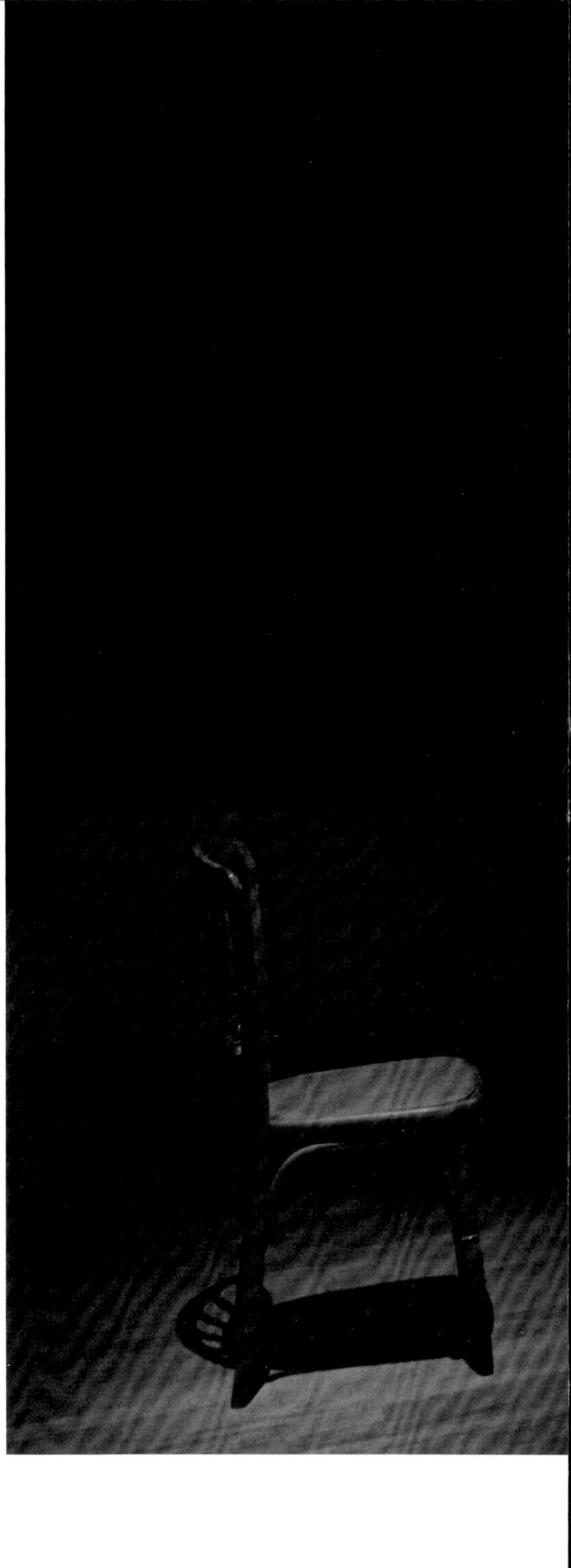

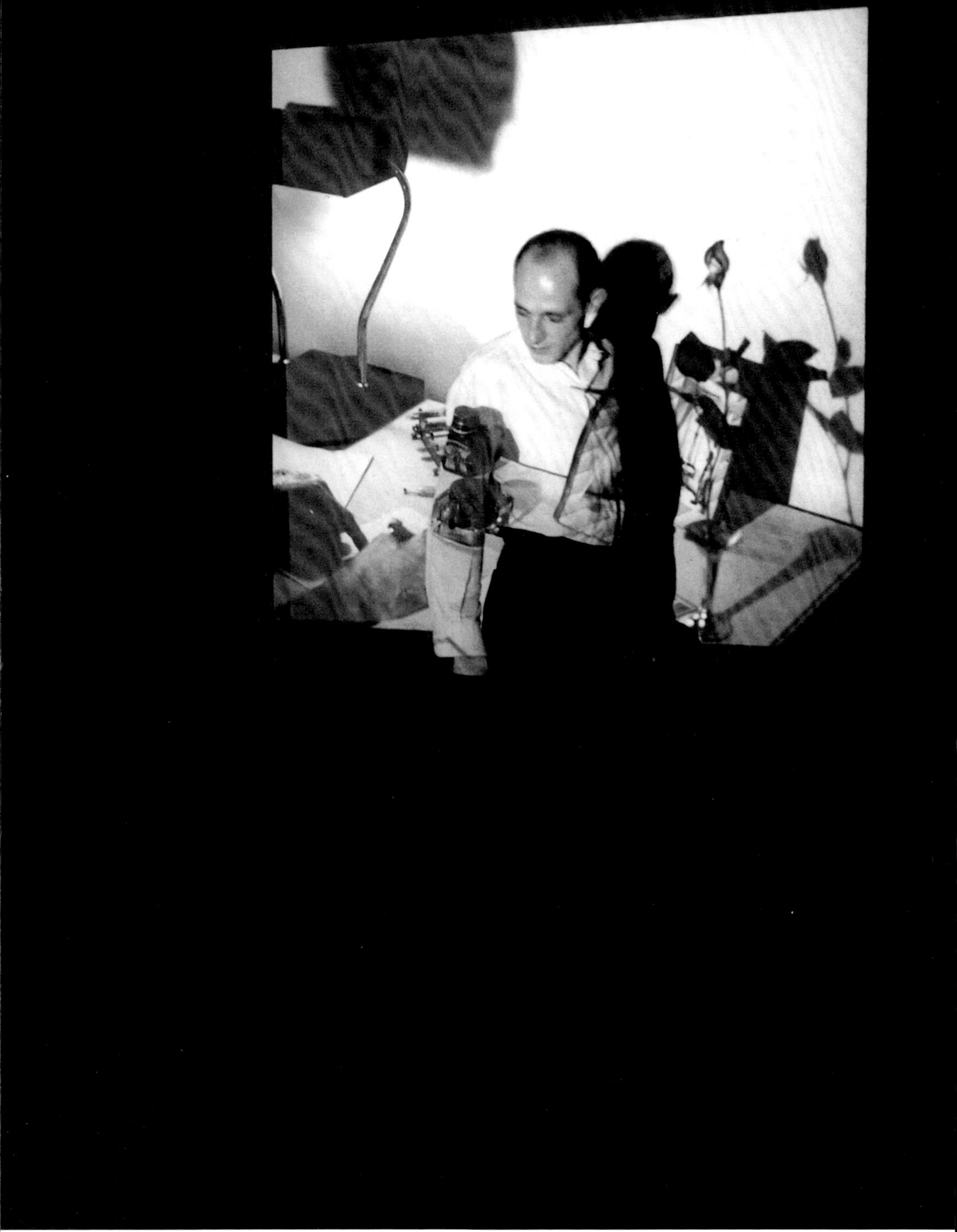

fig. 7 Marc Camille Chaimowicz, *Partial Eclipse…* (1981—2006): performance still, performance and installation at Tate Britain, London, 1981. Courtesy Cabinet, London and the artist.

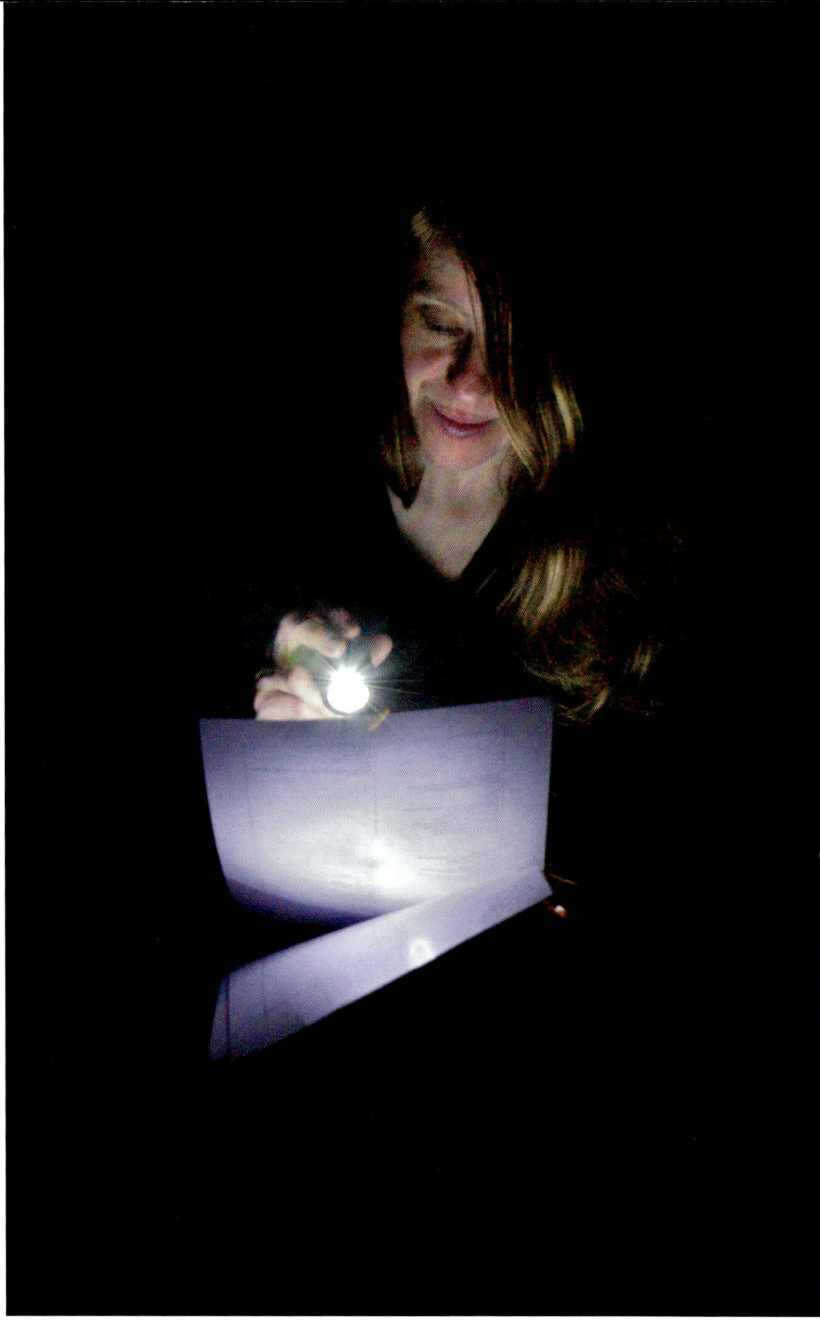

fig. 8 (above) Clare Gasson, *The Traveller Walking Walking Walking Through* (2010): performance documentation. Photo: Sam Nightingale.

fig. 9 Clare Gasson, *Performers (manifestos)* from *The River* (2011): sculptures made during the Women's Art Library bursary April—Nov 2011. Photo: Althea Greenan.

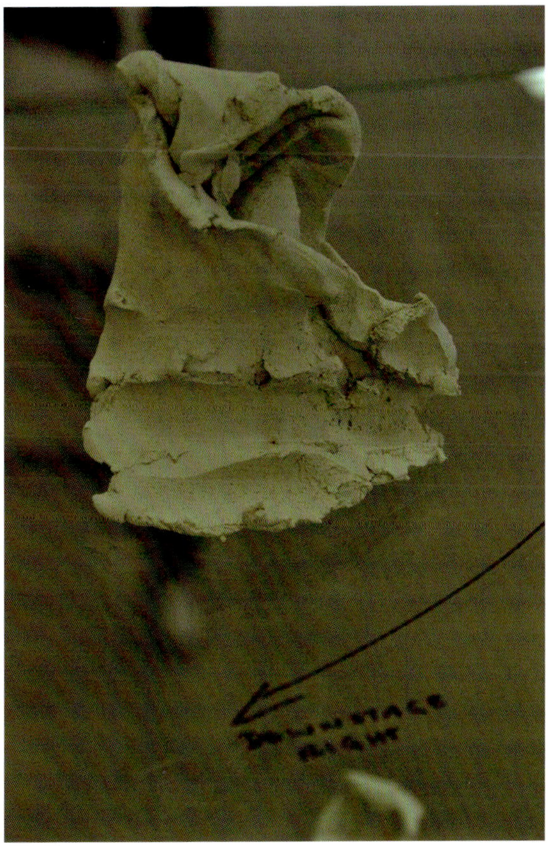
DOWNSTAGE
RIGHT

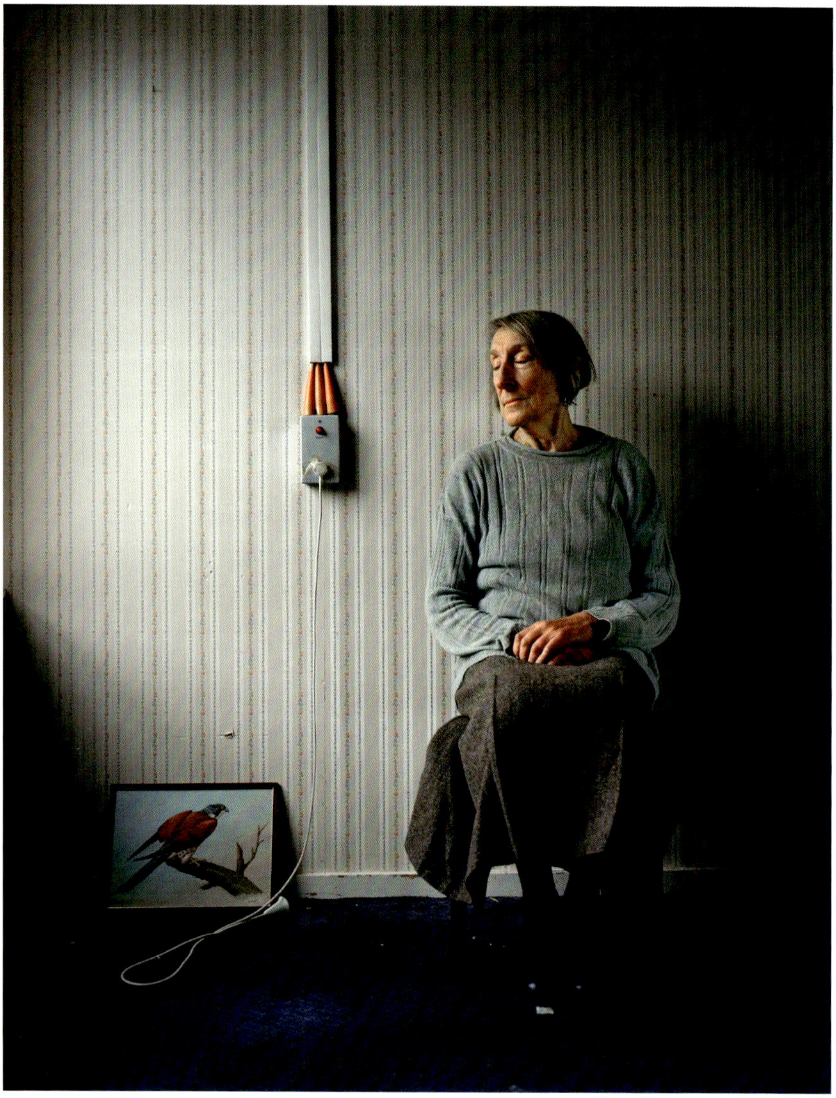

fig. 10 (above) Beatrice Gibson with Adam Broomberg and Oliver Chanarin, *1. Voice G. (Deep, deliberate, polite, careful not to interrupt. Pensive, dreamy, attentive to other voices. Stoic.)*, (2010): photograph.

fig. 11 (right) Beatrice Gibson with Adam Broomberg and Oliver Chanarin, *2. Voice B. (Shifting tones, from shrill to base. Consistent pace and tone in monologue sections. Hearing impaired. At times isolated, articulated as if a solo, independent...)*, (2010): photograph.

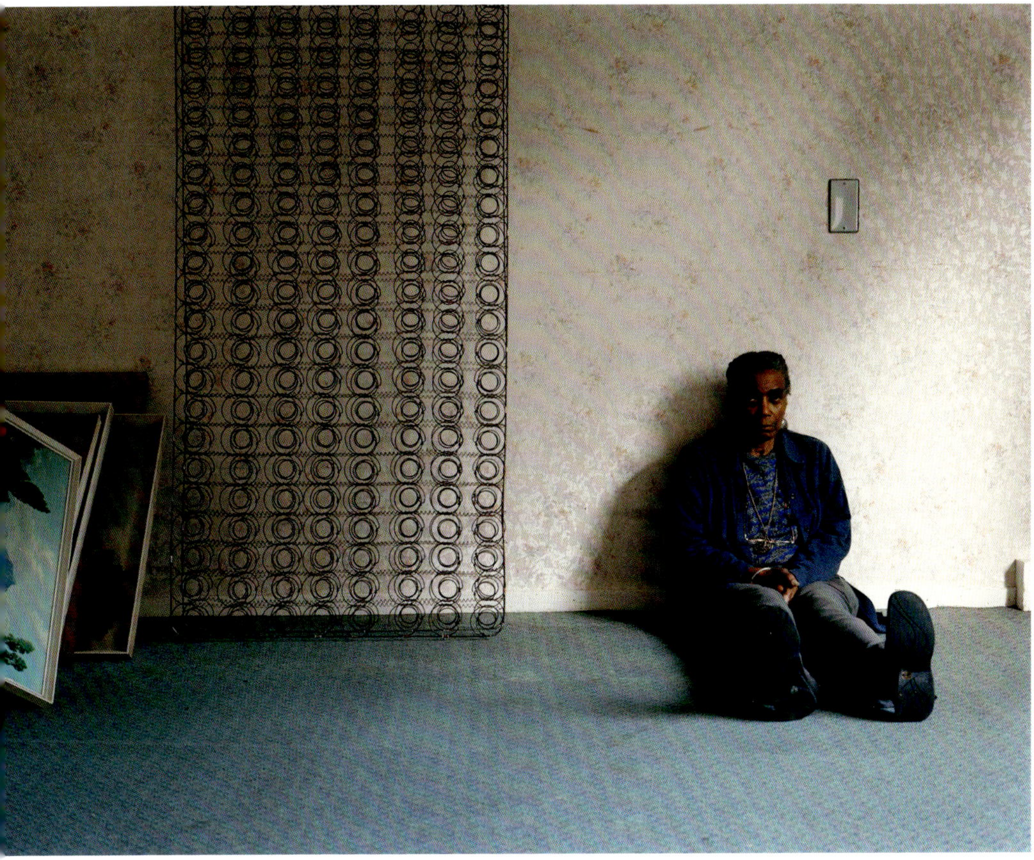

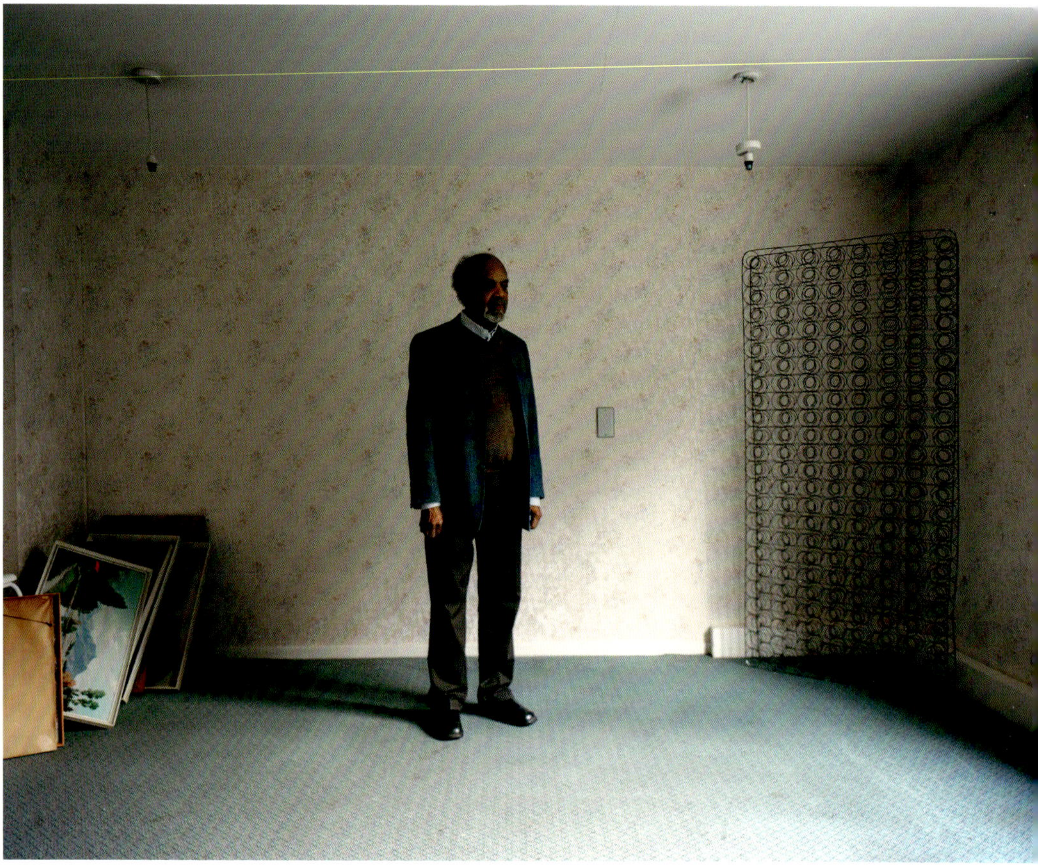

fig. 12 (above) Beatrice Gibson with Adam Broomberg and Oliver Chanarin, *3. Voice A. (Low, shifting volumes, from loud to mumbling. Fast but fumbling. Bursts of certainty, becoming mechanical, distracted, fragmented. Fluctuating coherence...)*, (2010): photograph.

fig. 13 (right) Beatrice Gibson with Adam Broomberg and Oliver Chanarin, *4. Voice H. (Slurry. Gurgly. Loses ends of words. Fast. Colloquial, chummy, cheeky. Consistent volume and tone irrespective of content. Unaffected. Unbothered. Hollow)*, (2010): photograph.

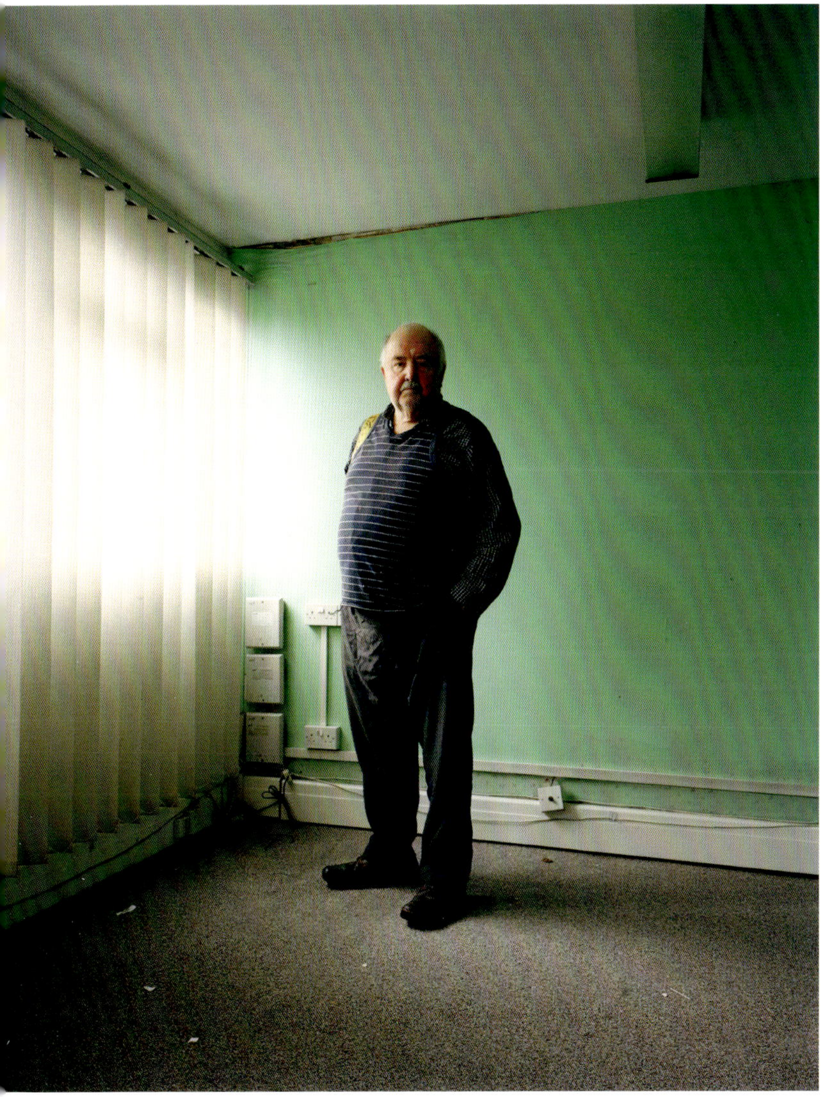

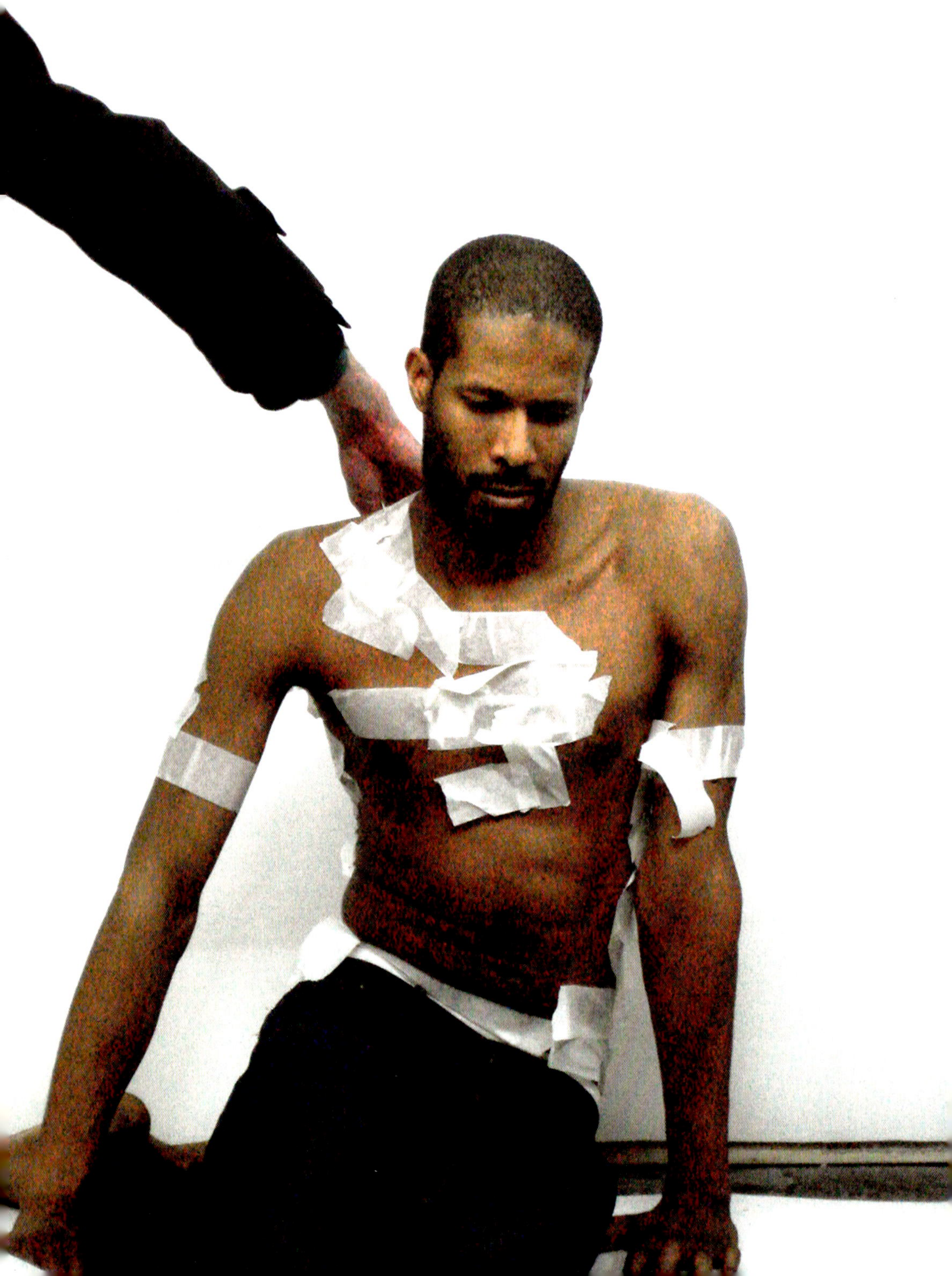

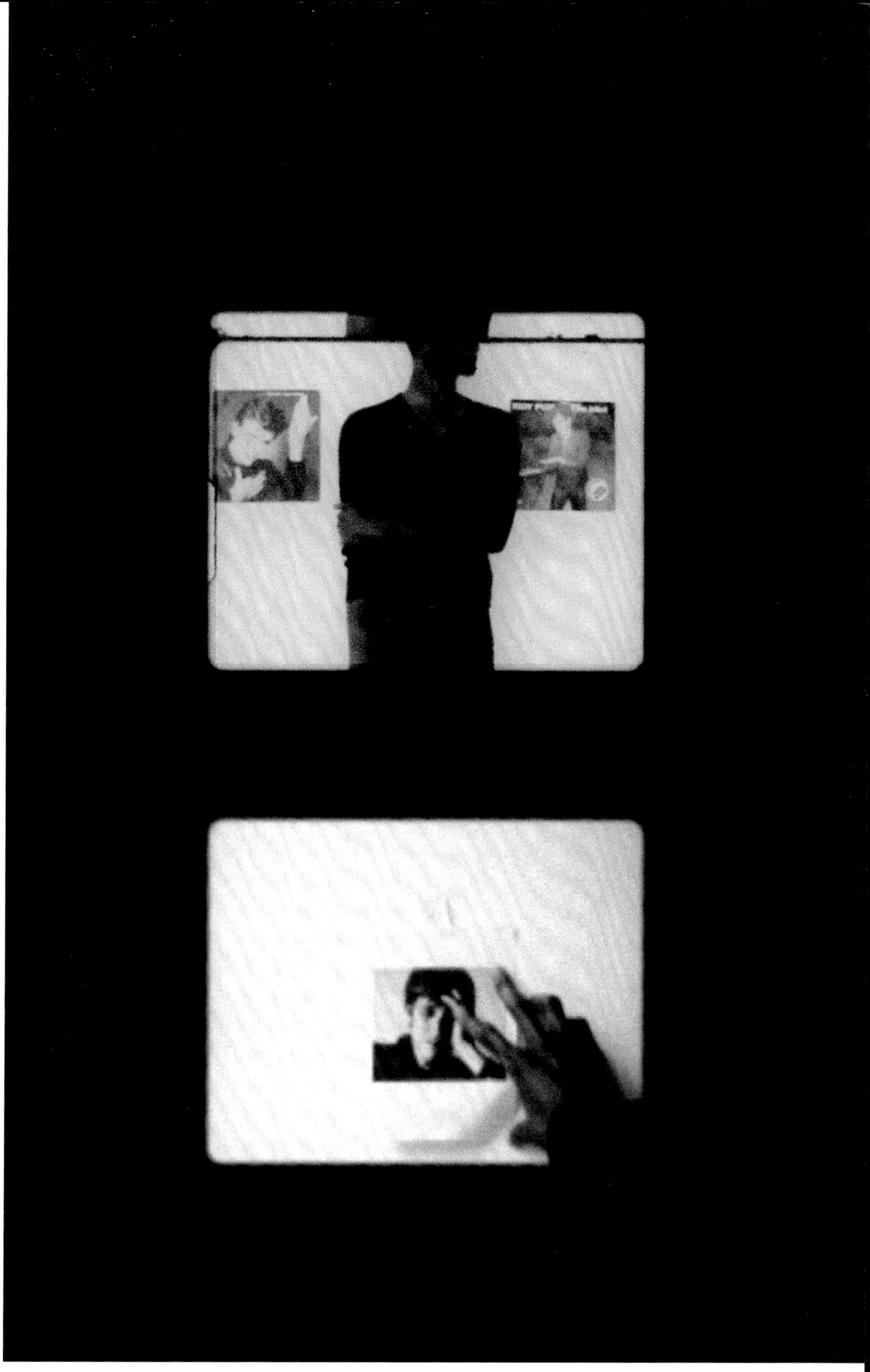

fig. 15 (above) Jimmy Robert, *L'Education Sentimentale* (2005): 35mm film stills.

fig. 14 (left) Jimmy Robert, *Figure de Style* (2008): performance documentation.

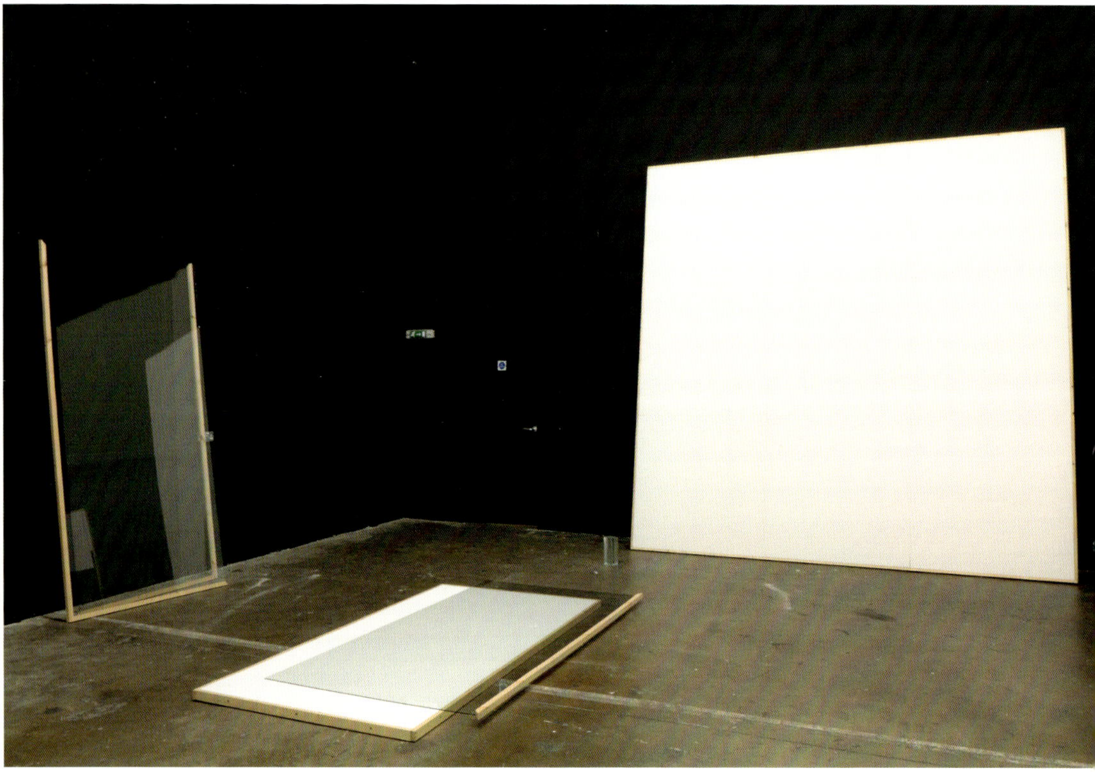

fig. 16 Yael Davids, *Learning to Imitate in Absentia* (2011): performance documentation, Picture This. Photo: Stuart Bunce.

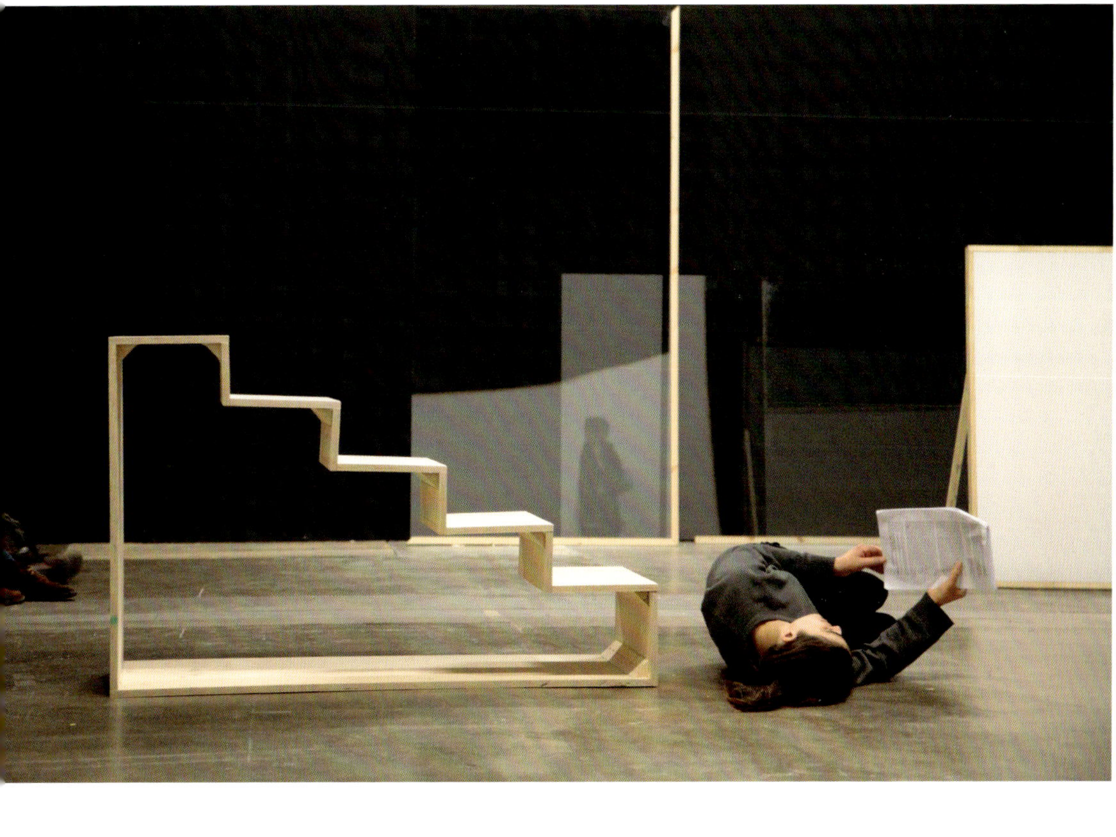

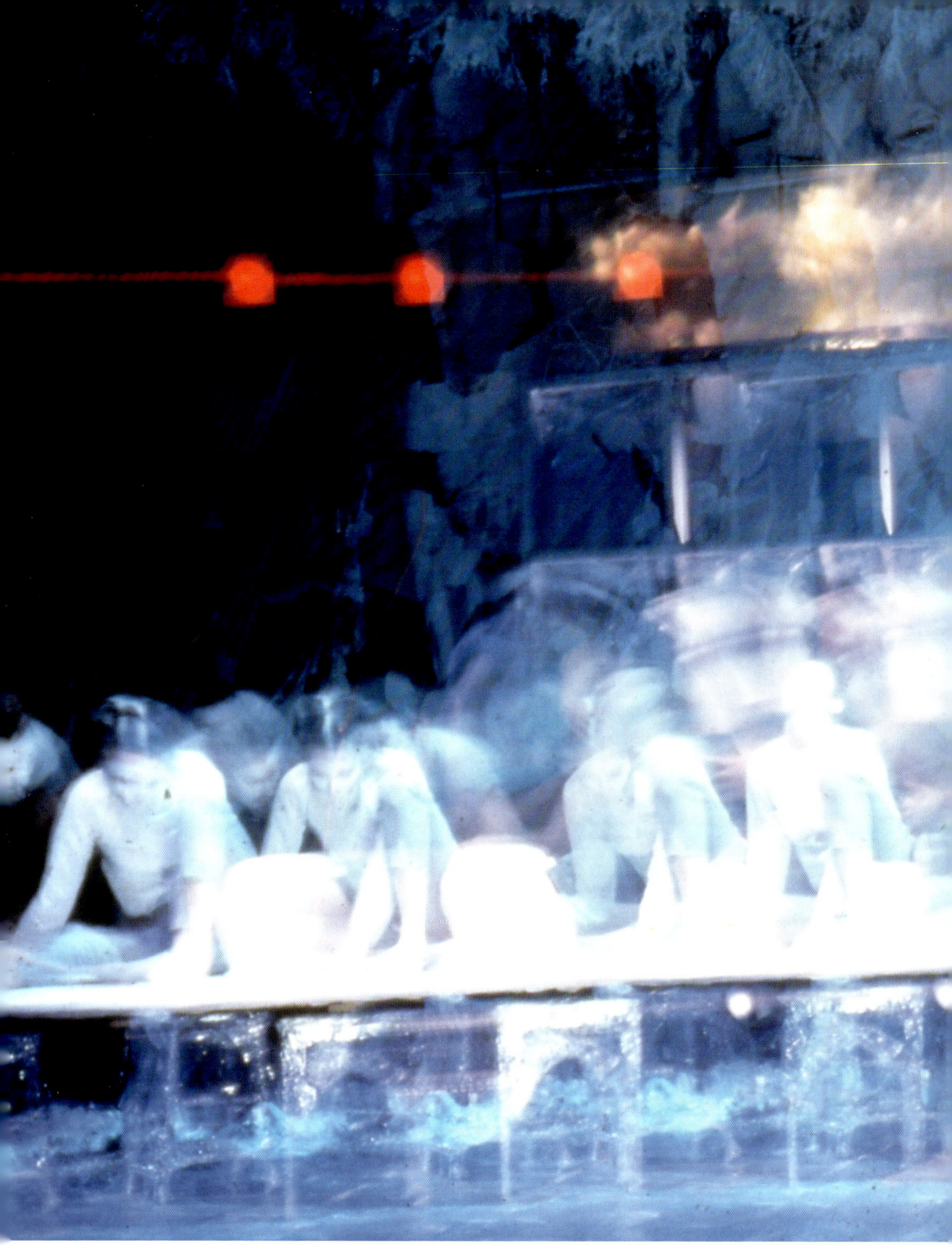

fig. 17 Carolee Schneemann, *Snows* (1967): Kinetic Theatre, Performance at Martinique Theater, NYC. Photo: Herbert Migdoll ©Carolee Schneemann.

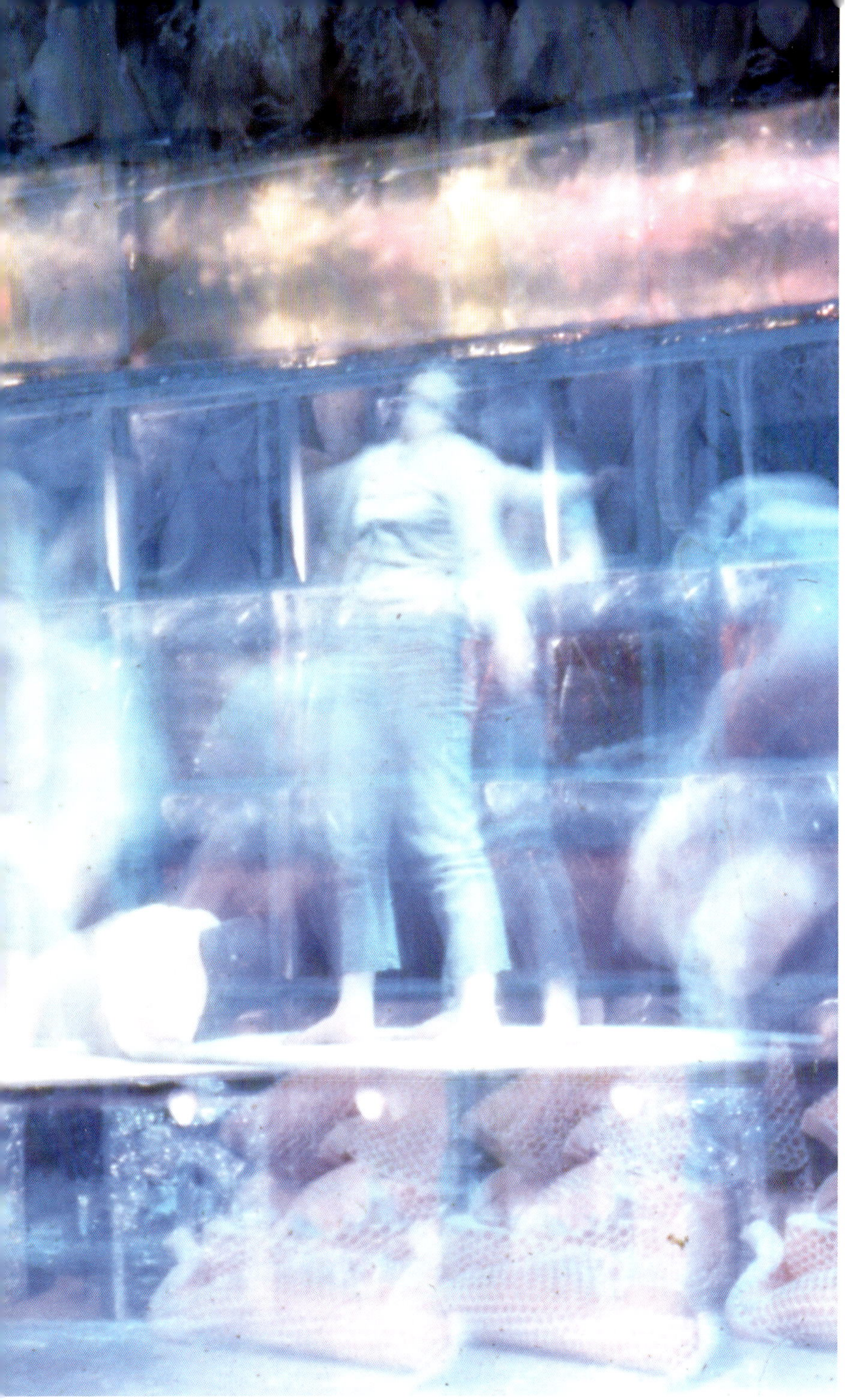

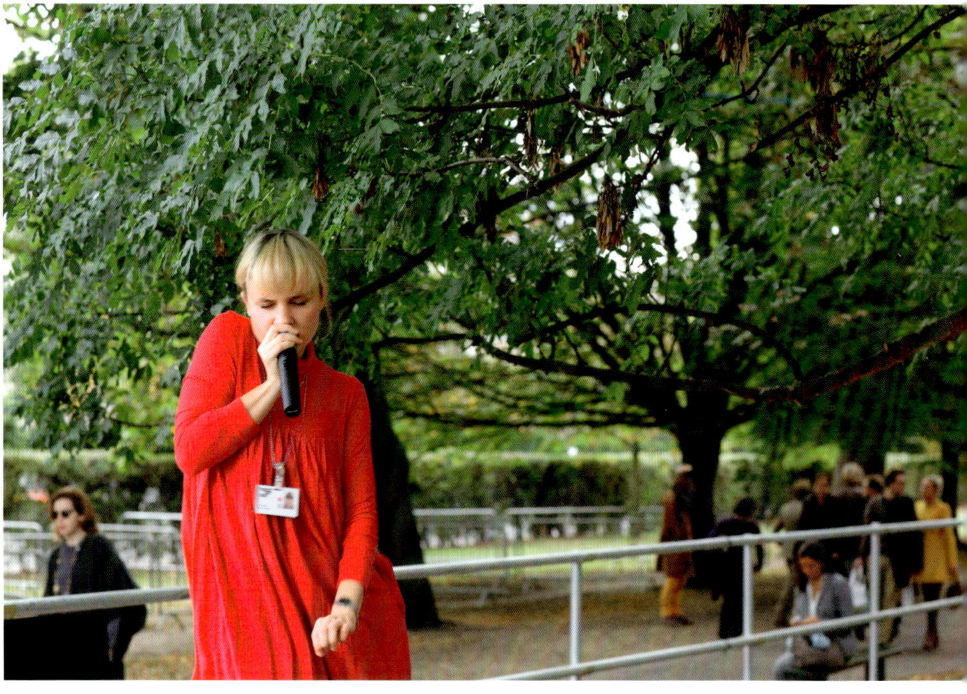

fig. 18 Cara Tolmie, *Myriad Mouth Line* (2011): performance documentation.
Commissioned and produced by Frieze Foundation for Frieze Projects 2011. Photo: Polly Braden.

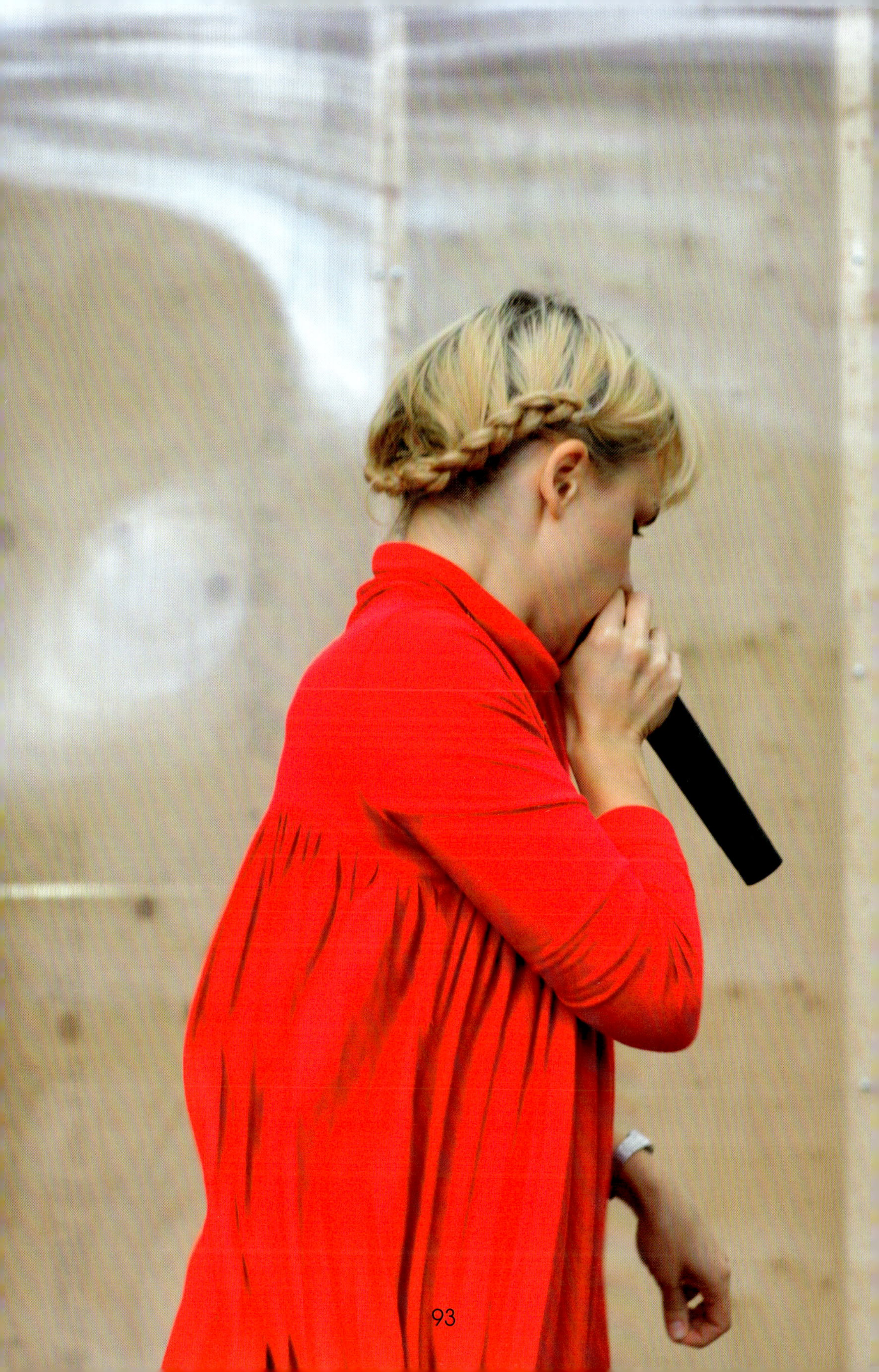

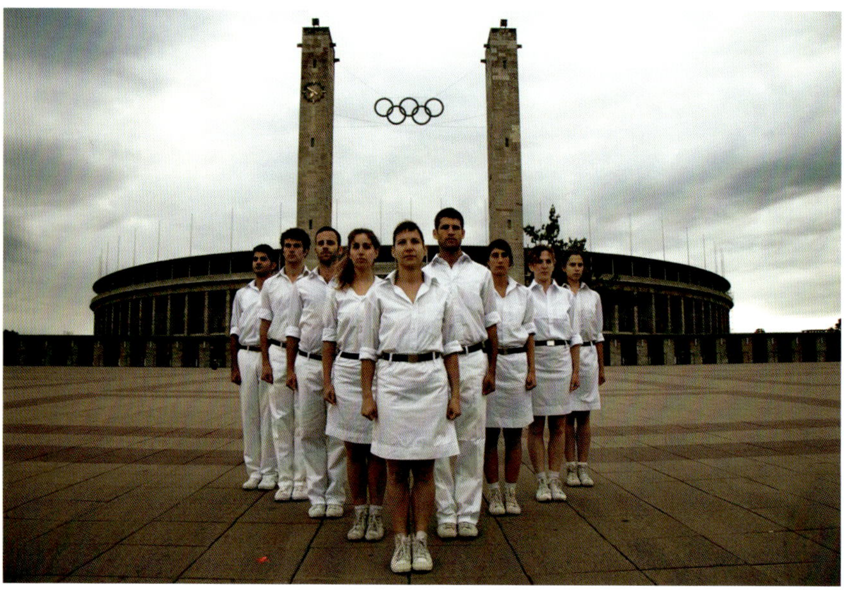

fig. 19 (above) Public Movement, *Performing Politics for Germany, Olympic Stadium* (2009), Berlin: documentation of performance. Photo: David Schmidt. Produced by Hebbel Am Ufer Theater.

fig. 20 (right) Crime (1977): publicity stills, taken at BART stations in San Francisco. ©James Stark.

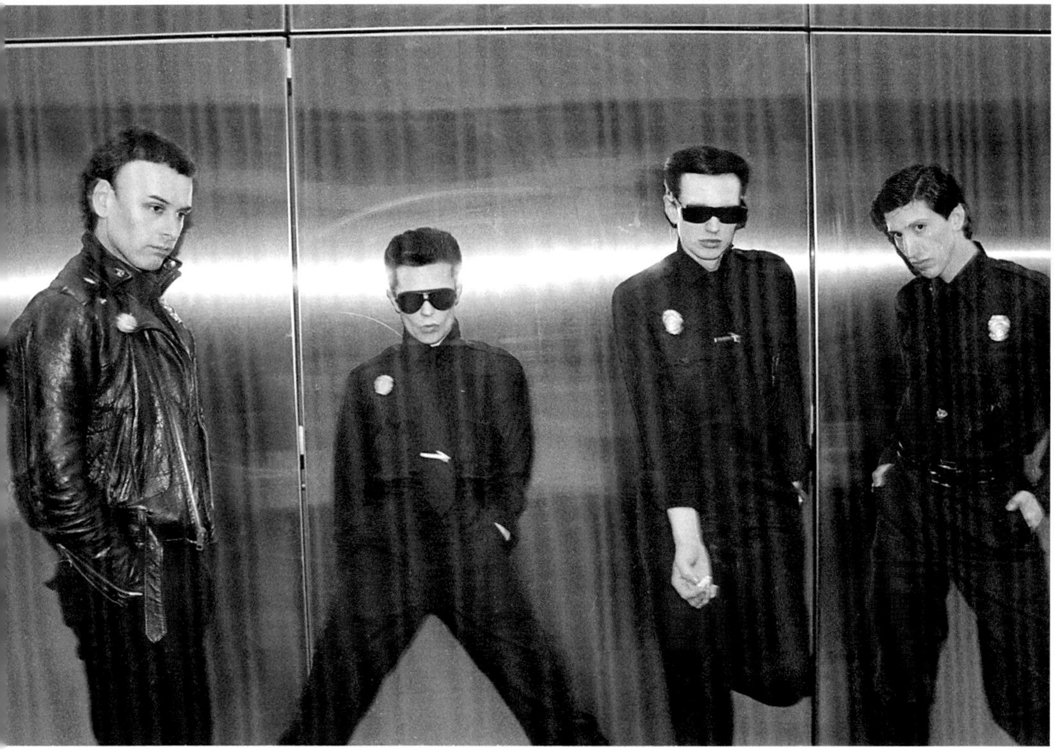

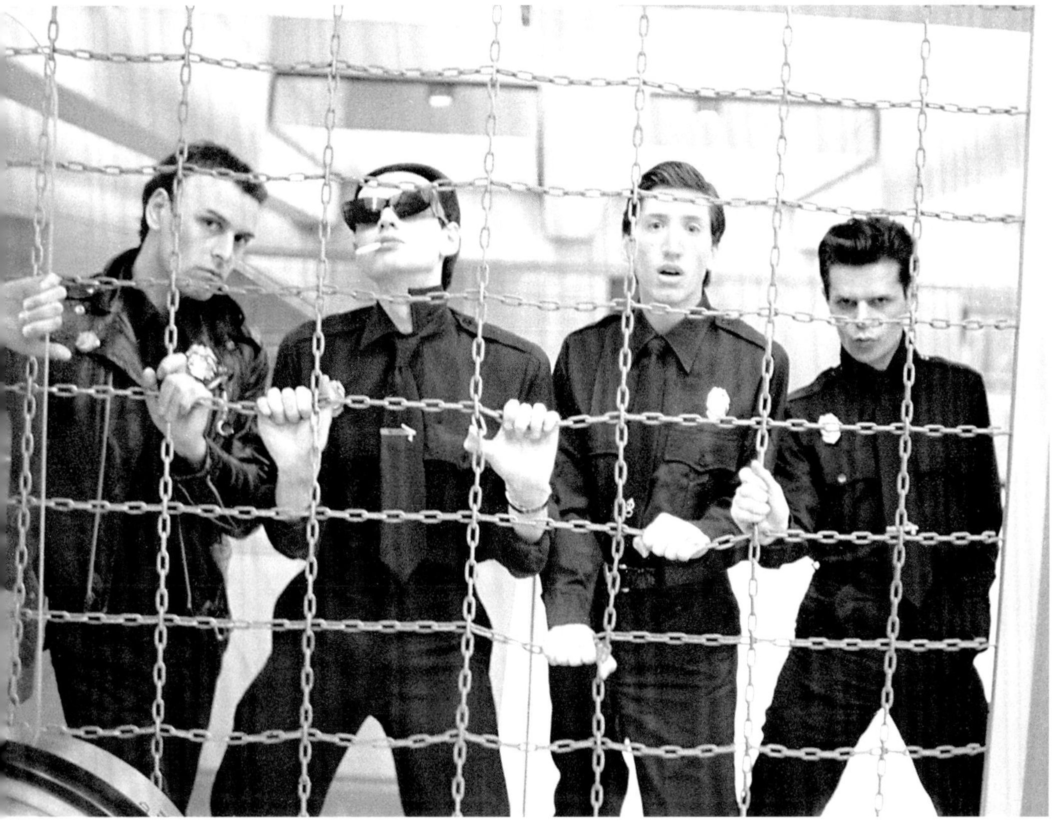

Treatise on Movement was presented by Media Art Bath as part of *A Theatre To Address: a festival of textual form / concrete / material / scripted / performed*, held at Arnolfini, Bristol in June 2010, and curated by Bridget Crone.

Treatise on Movement

BEATRICE GIBSON

INTRODUCTION

I'm going to talk a little today about the script and the score and some issues
I have around them and in between them.
I'm going to try to demonstrate as well as to talk,
or perhaps to demonstrate through talking,
not really to talk about
but to talk around.
But maybe its better to just...

8th Feb '63

Notation is a way of making people move. If you lack others, like aggression or persuasion. The notation should do it. This is the most rewarding aspect of work on a notation. Trouble is: just as you find your sounds are too alien, intended 'for a different culture', you make the same discovery about your beautiful notation: no one is willing to understand it. No one moves.[1]

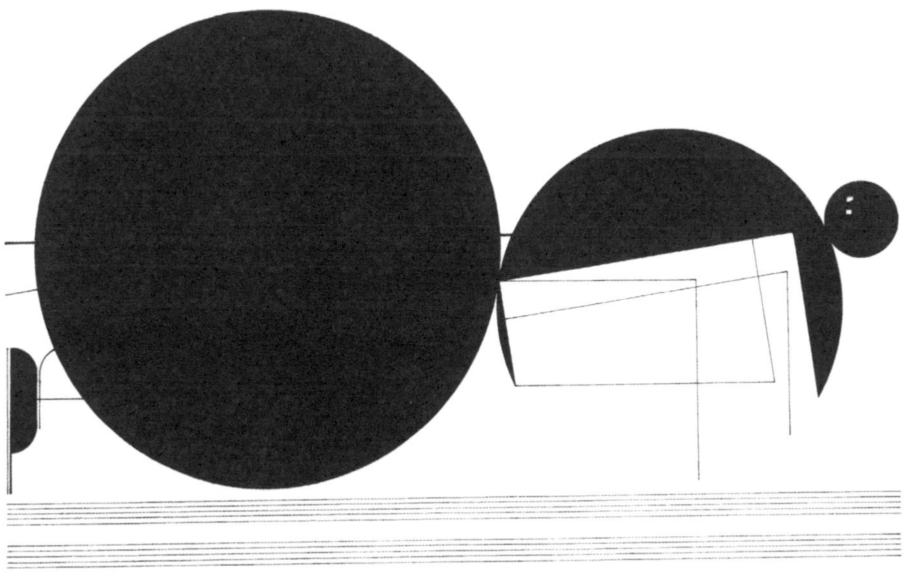

Treatise, Cornelius Cardew (1967), Gallery Upstairs Press, USA. Courtesy Edition Peters.

PROLOGUE

This is a score called *Treatise*.
Treatise was written by the experimental composer Cornelius Cardew between 1963-67.
It takes its name from Wittgenstein's *Tractatus Logico Philosophicus*, and consists of 193 pages, presenting an array of shapes that vary from the recognisably musical to the utterly abstract.

There aren't really any clear indications as to how to play *Treatise*.
Performers come together as a social group and through dialogue and consensus determine how it will be read
and what sounds it will produce.

The task of the players is essentially to assign sounds to symbols,
deciding what kind of sounds and how one might differentiate them.
Some strategies might include:
assigning meaning to a symbol's location relative to the centre line,
assigning specific symbols to a specific player,
how to play (as opposed to what to play),
associating a symbol with silence or with listening or with another player.

Over the years a collective oral discourse has grown up around the work,
emerged out of its continued playing.
Much after its original publication
and with a certain reluctance,
Cardew wrote an accompanying handbook
with some ideas, drawn from this discourse,
and of course, to a degree, his own intentions,
as to how it might be played.

The politics of *Treatise* and other graphic scores of its kind
is that they are models of action.
They are models, in other words, for making people move.
Fundamentally, what they sought to do, was to challenge the rigid hierarchy
between composer and performer,
to foreground increased levels of participation on the part of the performer
by blowing apart his or her musical habit.

Treatise and others like it
proposed a radical new model of reading,
in which the participant was transformed
from passive implementer of pre-ordained sounds

into co-author of a landscape of potential sound.
In the act of doing so
they transformed music making,
or the making of music
into a radical social act.
But maybe I'll just play you a little.

(*Treatise* plays, 4'54" mins)

And so it goes, for another 190 pages or so.
That was Prague in 1967, The Quax Ensemble.

EXPOSITION

Wellesley Road Care
home, Camden.
Voice A

One, Space
of moon landing)

INT, Wellesley Road Care
home, Camden.
Voice B

Scene One, Space
(Footage of moon landing)

I can't hear...... I can't hear . . . . I don't know what their talking about.

There's somebody talking. I'm deaf.

INT, Wellesley Road Care
home, Camden.
Voice C

Scene One, Space
(Footage of moon landing)

Look at that. What's that. There's a big black beetle. Running. Across the floor.

By his left foot. Left foot. Right foot.

May I say something. I can't say its been a life changing event. I just. . . recall seeing it . . .I saw it . . in black and white. After that there were so many B-movies made. Made with directors and so on. I became totally bored. Bored. I put it out my mind.

There were all the plastic balloons. And they were floating up and down in space as it were, weren't they? (Cough. Cough)

INT, Wellesley Road Care
home, Camden.
Voice D

Scene One, Space
(Footage of moon landing)

Yes Yes

I'll try anything once.

The thing is . . .

I was in Germany, dancing

Germany

INT, Wellesley Road Care
home, Camden.
Voice E

Scene One, Space
(Footage of moon landing)

That's amazing. I remember that.

I never found out what happened but there was a man who went and walked on it wasn't there?

Germans. He didn't go to Germany.

It's amazing that we actually were able to get up there.

Yes . . .

I would have liked to have gone up there. It must be fascinating. We should be able to get up there. We seem to fly around. We're so advanced now compared to what we were years ago. I would love to go.

INT, Wellesley Road Care
home, Camden.
Voice F

Scene One, Space
(Footage of moon landing)

The man who was walking on the moon. 1969.

The best thing to come out of that was the frying pan. The non-sticky frying pan. You put your eggs in. You put your, your, er lard whatever it may be and it never stuck to the pan. It never stuck to the pan. They invented that from the moon. They, got it from the stones of the moon.

They never went again because there was that much going on down here. Murders every ten seconds of the day or drugs and all the rest of it.

INT, Wellesley Road Care
home, Camden.
Voice G

Scene One, Space
(Footage of moon landing)

It takes . . . . courage,

Unrealistic it seemed. It was almost like a vision in a dream, I felt, that I couldn't quite make it reality, it took me some time to do so, when it was talked on the radio and on television, when they enlarged on it, then I was able to grasp, step by step what went on because the landing itself and ... people like myself didn't know what to make of it and how they got there.

INT, Wellesley Road Care
home, Camden.
Voice H

Scene One, Space
(Footage of moon landing)

Beatrice Gibson and George Clark, *The Future's Getting Old Like The Rest Of Us* (2010): script.

Lately, I've been trying to think about making films as an exercise
in making people move.
I've been trying to use the score as a paradigm for production of sorts,
trying to think these things or repurpose this idea of making people move,
through the medium of film.
More specifically perhaps I've been
trying to think these issues through the script,
trying to make the score and script have tea together, as it were.

This is a page from the script for *The Future's Getting Old Like The Rest Of Us* (2010). 8 vertical columns spaced horizontally across the page,
reflect 8 voices articulating themselves simultaneously. But maybe I'll just play you a little.

(Prologue from the *The Future's Getting Old Like The Rest Of Us*, 2'11)

The script for *The Future's Getting Old Like The Rest Of Us* was a collaboration with critic and curator George Clark,
alongside the residents of an old people's home in Camden.

Over a period of roughly five months, we set up a series of weekly discussions that were very tightly structured or composed.
These sessions were prompted by a series of questions, determined in advance,
so as to produce quite a specific or directed form of speech.
A list of questions like:

What will London be like in 100 years?
Will the current economic crisis change the future?
Are your memories images, sounds or words?
Are you worried about forgetting?

Alongside this we showed films, images and sounds,
again as compositional prompts.

The results of these sessions were then recorded, captured and transcribed.
The transcriptions then edited into a script,
and structured formally, in fact
(in terms of the 8 columns, the 8 voices)
by another text;
a book called *House Mother Normal*, written in 1972
by the late British experimental author B.S Johnson.
The final script, the script you see here, was then given over to others,
to actors,

to re-articulate,
and restage for film.

So, the way I think of the script is not as single object on paper,
the result of a single person's labour
or as what one might conceivably call a commodity object,
but as a much wider thing,
as a methodology in and of itself,
that has to do with a social process and the instigation of that,
that has to do with making people move.

The way I think of the script, my idea of the script,
has to do with a translation of something already uttered into something else,
as a collection of sayings or a quotation of voices,
that in their re-writing or re-articulation or re-staging
become something other,
something fictional perhaps.

The way I think of the script
is not simply as a static archive of speech prompted or uttered,
but as methodology,
as an alibi if you like for making people move.

And by movement, I mean more than simply
the literal choreographing of a physical action,
I mean in the instigation of a social process,
the moving that goes on, in and around the entirety
of the process of making the script,
from the collective construction of its content,
to its subsequent re-articulation and the effects of that re-articulation.

DEVELOPMENT

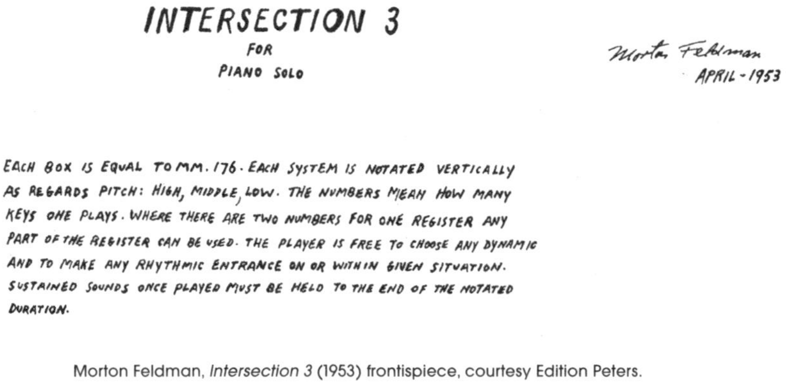
INTERSECTION 3
FOR
PIANO SOLO
Morton Feldman
APRIL - 1953

EACH BOX IS EQUAL TO MM. 176. EACH SYSTEM IS NOTATED VERTICALLY AS REGARDS PITCH: HIGH, MIDDLE, LOW. THE NUMBERS MEAN HOW MANY KEYS ONE PLAYS. WHERE THERE ARE TWO NUMBERS FOR ONE REGISTER ANY PART OF THE REGISTER CAN BE USED. THE PLAYER IS FREE TO CHOOSE ANY DYNAMIC AND TO MAKE ANY RHYTHMIC ENTRANCE ON OR WITHIN GIVEN SITUATION. SUSTAINED SOUNDS ONCE PLAYED MUST BE HELD TO THE END OF THE NOTATED DURATION.

Morton Feldman, *Intersection 3* (1953) frontispiece, courtesy Edition Peters.

(Reads from John Cage's *Silence*)

'This is a lecture on composition which is indeterminate in respect to its composition...'

This is *Intersection 3*

(*Intersection 3* plays, 3'14")

So I have been trying to think about the script as being some kind of attempt
to make a person move.
And I've been trying to think through this movement
in terms of the instigation of a social process.

This idea of social process is about something more though
than simply the gathering of a social body
in order to collectively construct something
within or without a given compositional framework.

This idea of social process, of movement, also pertains to something
not quite so physical, so literal.
It has to do with moving in a different way,
with being asked to move,
or to read,
or to act,
in a different way from before.

The graphic score as a kind of writing
implies a radically different form of reading or participation or labour.
It has something to do with a working backwards perhaps,
with a labour in reverse,
with an unbuilding
or an unlearning.

The graphic score as a kind of writing
seems to me to activate the reader
in a way that arrests
or that blows apart
the conventional understanding of reading as a passive act.
It has to do with a re-assessment of how we read.
I'll read someone who articulates it better than me.

(Reads from Michel De Certeau, *Reading as Poaching*)

'What has to be put in question is unfortunately not this division of labor....'

What I'm trying to say then,
or rather to think out loud,
is how the graphic score and how the script might have do with
or have the potential for
a kind of poetics of activation.

We had three rehearsals before shooting *The Future's Getting Old*
With 9 people speaking more or less simultaneously and the cost of 16mm stock
we couldn't really afford to have not worked out a system in advance.
I presented each of the actors with 21 pages of A3, consisting,
as you saw and heard
of 8 vertical columns placed horizontally along the page.
My instructions, or my direction perhaps, was to stress the nature of the script
as a guideline for action,
as a guideline for when one might come in and at what point.
With 9 voices coinciding
it would of course be impossible to hear anything like a cue,
and that wasn't really the logic of the thing either.
I explained my background, my interest in the score,
I explained how essentially I was interested in the quotation of voice
in the musicality of speech.
It didn't matter to me exactly when someone came in or at what point,
it mattered more that a kind of vocal music took hold,
that the delivery veered between being semantically comprehensive,
and being something more like music,
that it veered,
in other words, between speech and noise.

But my point is this.
I had imagined the actors would immediately find this coherent, liberating,
obvious.
They didn't.
They resisted it forcefully.
They had to unlearn sixty years of doing something a particular way.

(Audio clip from the set *Actors revolt, Actors laughing* 5'40")

Personally I think the results were amazing,
in terms of being there, seeing it happen.
Whether they did I don't know.
At any rate it made them laugh.

Morton Feldman once said,

'I never understood what rules I was supposed to learn, and what rules I was supposed to break'.

Maybe the laughter came from the vertigo of incomprehension.

DISINTEGRATION

TRIOS (WHITE ON WHITE)

Robert Ashley (1963)

The nature of these trios will be made clearer, if the performer can imagine them to have been printed in the following manner:

TRIO I - The three matrixes of numbers should occupy (by super-imposition) the same 8½"by 8½"area at the top of an 8½"by 11" sheet of stiff, off-white paper. The numbers should be block-characters occupying the major part of adjacent 21mm by 18mm areas. The characters of one matrix should be embossed lightly on the paper. The characters of another matrix should be printed in white, heavily textured, matte ink, slightly "raised" on the paper. The characters of the third matrix should be printed in a white, glossy ink. Instructions should be printed on the bottom portion of the page in a complementary white ink.

TRIO II - The instructions for all players should be printed in white on a single 8½"by 11" sheet of off-white paper. A printed 8½"by 11" sheet of off-white card stock should be provided from which the set of ten performance-cards can be cut. One series of performance-card numbers should be printed in heavily textured, matte white ink. The other series of numbers should be printed in a glossy white ink.

TRIO III - Instructions and text should be embossed on a single sheet (8½"by 11") of stiff, off-white paper. This embossing should be printed over with a glossy white ink.

Robert Ashley, *Trios (White on White)* (1963), first page, instructions. Courtesy of the composer.

This is a score by Robert Ashley, called *Trios (White on White)*, written in 1963. The part that excites me is really the sentence,

'The nature of these trios will be made clearer, if the performer can imagine them to have been printed in the following way.'

In others words performers must first and foremost
imagine the printing of the score,
then fabricate it,
gather together a band,

delegate how the score will be read,
and only then collectively interpret it.
A graphic notation is not complete until it's read by a reader.
Contrary to conventional notation perhaps,
it's not an image of sound that exists already
but rather has to be translated into musical activity.
more than being read, the score is modified,
as De Certeau put it, in the act of being read;
it has to be interpreted,
translated,
made to sound.

A graphic score calls into question then
how one might interpret an imagined language.
When this language is translated its not definitive,
it doesn't cancel out the possibility of other translations.
As my friend the composer Alex Waterman says,
'A graphic score is a map of an imaginary territory.'
In other words it deploys imagination as a social principle,
it goes beyond being an exact representation of a said or a seen thing
to being a diagram of a possible world.

So rather than representing reality, notation intervenes in it,
its role is dynamic and creative.
Its job, is the job of fiction.
As Bob says,

'Notation is a bigger idea because it has to work in two ways. It means not only the possibility of the transcription of writing, in whatever form or system, but equally the possibility of something being re-created from the writing.'

So what I'm tying to say
or trying to get at
orientates around this idea of imagination
of fiction
as another kind of movement.

I think today we understand fiction in a very different way from how we used to.
I think today we quite clearly understand
and see
and witness
fiction, working formally if you like,
as cultural product or as a labour.

I think we understand fiction not simply as the construction of imaginary stories,
but experience it
as a labour,
as an active projection
that has to do with a re-description, a re-framing or a re-staging of the world.
In other words,
we understand how it operates actively in the world
how it has a projective capacity
and how it can open up other worlds,
how that can be wonderful, in that we are suddenly enabled to suddenly see the world differently
and how it can be dangerous
in terms of Bush and Blair fictionalising our landscapes
within a framework of terror
and that having very real and very concrete effects.

So I think we understand fiction today, again, as
not simply the construction of imaginary stories,
but as an active force, that has to do with
a re-framing or re-alignment of a given landscape, social reality, object or thing.

So fiction,
in fact
can be said to effect a kind of *dissensus*,
not in the sense of two people having an argument
but in the sense of introducing different models of reality into a given landscape,
different descriptions of reality,
that challenge and contrast with a singular or consensual view of that reality.
Dissensus can perhaps be aligned with a kind of poly-vocality,
in the sense of introducing the possibility of multiple worlds
or multiple perspectives on the world.

But to go from the abstract to the concrete,
my experience of transcribing the conversations in the old people's home,
of listening to them, recording them, capturing them and writing them down
is that they do, they did, become something very different,
something fictionalised,
simply in the sense that a copy of something is not the same as the original.

And my experience of working with actors to re-perform the script,
is that a kind of removal does takes place,
the aesthetic comes in,
those conversations or that speech has been abstracted,

removed,
made beautiful perhaps
and so we don't smell the piss anymore,
or see wrinkles quite in the same way.
We see them differently,
hear them differently,
feel them differently;
we experience the real in strangely heightened or perhaps oddly detached way.

So I suppose my idea of fiction,
in relation to the script,
or in relation to the scripting of the real,
is that it begins to function as a kind of estrangement device, in a Brechtian sense,
as something that might allow us to re-describe or re-frame the world
in a way that allows us to see it differently.
Movement in this sense is about a shift in meaning,
a shift in how we see and feel the world.

Here's the epilogue.

CODA

(Epilogue from *The Future's Getting Old Like The Rest Of Us.* 6'46")

ENDNOTES

(1) Cornelius Cardew, 'Treatise: working notes', *Treatise Handbook*, first published by Edition Peters, Hinrichsen Edition, Ltd, 1971. Reprinted in *Cornelius Cardew, a reader* ed. Edwin Prevost, published by Copula - an imprint of Matchless Recordings and Publishing, 2006.

Moving Poses / Arresting Feeling: Jimmy Robert's *L'Education Sentimentale*

DOMINIC ANDREW PATERSON

(Photo: powerless to say what is obvious. The birth of literature.)

__ Roland Barthes, *Mourning Diary*(1)

To touch with tact is to touch without touching that which does not let itself be touched: to embrace eyes, in a word (or in several words, and the word always brings to your ear the modest reserve of a kiss on the mouth). To touch as tact is, thanks to you, because of you, to break with immediacy, with the immediate given wrongly associated with touch and on which all bets are always placed...

__ Jacques Derrida, *On Touching - Jean-Luc Nancy*(2)

fig. 15 __ After a flurry of leader which makes the materiality of film palpable from the start, Jimmy Robert's *L'Education Sentimentale* (2005, 35mm, silent, 4'45") begins with a short sequence a little over 20 seconds long, shot in black and white, in which we see the artist with his back to the camera. He faces a short text written by hand on the otherwise blank wall in front of him. The text consists of two sentences, the first a plaintive announcement, the second either an injunction or a plea. 'I'm too sad to tell you', the first sentence states. 'Don't leave me', the second implores. Each is direct in its mode of address but it is unclear to whom they are addressed: is it Robert, or the viewer, or perhaps a third party? Though the subject of these statements is ambiguous, the desperate sentiments they express have a particular resonance for any viewer familiar with the work of the Dutch-American artist Bas Jan Ader, for they are derived from the titles of two of his works. Robert begins the film, then, by confronting what has already been said in the art historical past.

Robert begins to efface the words, initially by scribbling over them with what appears to be charcoal and then by blurring the resultant marks with his right hand. When he steps back from this activity and walks out of frame, we see that three words have been left untouched. And we might read these three words as producing a new sentence, one that is perhaps a rejoinder to the emotional pressure of the previous statements, a resistance to the tragic tone they employ, or to the art historical narratives they conjure: 'don't tell me.' At this point the film cuts and we see Robert once again facing the same wall, which bears traces of the previous action now more thoroughly erased and with the sentence, 'I'm too sad to tell you', rewritten and legible once more. In a series of gestures with both palms now pressed to the wall moving elegantly but rapidly over the words, Robert erases them again but almost at once begins to rewrite – an act interrupted by a second abrupt cut which falls even as the first letter of the phrase is completed. From this series of inscriptions, erasures, re-inscriptions, out of a partial dialogue initiated and continued in words that do not originate with Robert, an 'I' – provisional, in process, liable to ghost-like appearances and disappearances – flashes momentarily into view.

This opening sequence makes a fitting introduction not only to the specific themes addressed in *L'Education Sentimentale* but also to the concerns of Robert's practice more generally. Its sense of a tactile apprehension of language and image, its precise but informal presentation of performed actions, and its grasping of the art historical past through direct references to the works or practices of others, are all qualities which recur throughout Robert's *oeuvre*. In that larger body of work, as in the introduction to *L'Education Sentimentale*, Robert questionsthe means by which subjectivity might viably be figured in language, performed actions, film, or indeed in any form of art today. As Robert has put it:

> *...occupying language, assimilating other forms to create one's own discourse, is one of many strategies we can use to affirm the existence of the individual subject. The question that remains is whether this individuality is real, and to what extent it enters into the system of valorization belonging to a given plastic language.* (3)

This essay follows *L'Education Sentimentale's* trajectory from the assimilation of various already existing forms to its staging of a subjectivity that is put into question, subjected to both erasure and inscription. That questioning will be read in particular through a distinctive feature found in several of Robert's works, an evocation of the tactile (with its intimations of direct contact and immediacy) that is deliberately entangled with the archived, mediated form of the performance document.

GRASPING THE PAST

While the erasure and re-inscription of such an emotive phrase as 'I'm too sad to tell you' might be affecting in its own right, it is lent greater resonance thanks to its place in the of Bas Jan Ader. Ader is famous for a small but influential body of work made in the early 1970s, including his attempt to sail single-handed across the Atlantic for a piece entitled entitled *In Search of the Miraculous* (1975), which resulted in his tragic disappearance at sea. Though Ader's work is referred to throughout *L'Education Sentimentale*, it is not, I think, the subject matter of Robert's film.(4) Rather, it provides a set of touchstones, artistic and physical gestures that Robert reworks or recodes. I will consider Robert's historical allusions in order to elucidate what it is that he with each, and how subjectivity emerges as the film's subject.

The first such touchstone in *L'Education Sentimentale* is found in the opening sequence already described, which explicitly references two of Ader's works: *Please Don't Leave Me* (1969), a photographed studio installation with the title hand-painted in large black letters on Ader's studio wall and illuminated by a spotlight affixed to a ladder, and *I'm Too Sad to Tell You* (1971). (5) This latter work was made in a number of forms, including a postcard featuring a photograph of the artist seemingly as inconsolable as the title would imply, with tears streaming down his face and his left hand raised to his head in an echo of a whole series of representations of melancholy, including, most famously, Albrecht Dürer's *Melencolia I* (1514).(6) The postcard was sent to a number of his friends, with no message but the date (September 13th 1970) and the title handwritten on the reverse. A photographic edition of the work was also produced with the text written over the bottom right of the image. In addition, Ader made three attempts at producing a filmed version, abandoning one effort in California and ultimately completing it in Amsterdam in 1971. In their detailed catalogue of Ader's work, Alexandra Blättler and Rein Wolfs describe the film as follows:

> *[Ader] is filmed frontally. His face, full of emotion, fills the screen. He pulls his hair and rubs his face. He snivels and tears show. He opens his mouth, rubs his eyes, lifts his head, blinks his eyes, grins, bends his head, curls his lip inward, bursts into tears,*

> *regains control, moves his tongue over his lips, keeps his head still, bends his head again, can't hold back his tears, turns his head to the left, shakes his head, curls his lip inward, puts a hand on his face and flicks his hair out of the way, nods, keeps his eyes closed and bursts into tears again.*(7)

Ader, in other words, performs the full range of conventional signs for despair in the film, a work which speaks of the unspeakable, of a unique moment of incommunicable sadness but does so through a clear evocation of the inherent iterability of a lexicon of feeling which can be reproduced and repeated, sincerely or otherwise, at different moments and in different places.

Jan Verwoert urges us to look beyond the seeming contradiction between 'real' expressions of sentiment and the performance and re-performance of the signs of such sentiment, and to see how *I'm Too Sad to Tell You* asks us to understand emotions: 'in conceptual, rhetorical and existential terms, without any of these aspects cancelling out the others.'(8) Ader, Verwoert argues: 'does not seek to deny or overcome the ready-made rhetorical quality of the motifs or genres he draws on. Rather it is precisely at the level of their rhetoricity that he discovers their potential.'(9) Verwoert's broader contention is that in Ader's work we see the protocols of conceptual art applied to the themes of romanticism, including the tragic quest (*In Search of the Miraculous*) and the creative potential of melancholy (*I'm Too Sad to Tell You*). Thus, true to the conceptual dimension of his approach, Ader withholds narrative explanation of why he is crying, and presents only documents of that state of affairs, reducing crying to its rhetorical essentials. But at the same time, the work really is affecting, Ader's tears do tell us that some things are too sad to be told, just as when he makes his romantic journey, he really does risk his life in an ocean crossing. For Verwoert, Ader uses conceptual art's *modus operandi* to test out what potential might remain in the now untimely romanticist attitude and to create works that are both critical and emotive, rhetorical and real.

In *L'Education Sentimentale* Robert similarly engages rhetoric and feeling, but not via the formal strategies of conceptualism or the sublime affects central to romanticism. Robert works instead through a rethinking of Ader's presentation of emotion in the wake of subsequent critical art and theory, and in terms of intersubjectivity rather than through the figure of the tragic hero as isolated individual. In interposing his own body between Ader's language and the camera's lens in the opening sequence of *L'Education Sentimentale* Robert already hints at this, as he also does in the extension of Ader's play with the shifting reference of personal pronouns (the way 'I,' 'me,' 'you' are dependent on the context of their enunciation for their meaning). That it is Robert who is the agent of both the erasure of these words and their re-inscription suggests that this might be an inner dialogue with imagined others upon whom the subject (any subject) depends for its own identity.[10]

A clearer example of this emphasis on the inter-subjective character of identity is perhaps to be found in the next sequence of *L'Education Sentimentale* in which Robert takes up a group of film works by Ader. In this sequence we see restaged versions of two of Ader's 'fall' films but we view them as if shot from the opposite position to that occupied by the camera in the originals. Whereas in Ader's *Fall II, Amsterdam* (1970) we see the artist from across a canal as he rounds a street corner on a bicycle, intentionally veering into the water as if to deliver the physical punchline to a slapstick movie joke, in Robert's film we see a cyclist poised on the edge of a canal, viewed from behind.[11] From out of shot, Robert calmly walks up to the cyclist, steadies the bicycle and allows its rider to tip gently over into his embrace as if to hold him back from the edge. The moment is held, emphasising the support one body gives the other, but nothing about its performance is dramatic. The effect is striking however: it is as though Robert has emerged, ghost-like, from within the depths of Ader's film but also, conversely, as if the insubstantial image of Ader on that film has become graspable, reachable. This play between the spectral and substantial is present in the film throughout, in fact, thanks to a number of colour shots which are interspersed in it, showing a silver-haired man, again filmed from behind, as if this could be a contemporary version of Ader had he somehow survived his ill-fated voyage in 1975. This counterfactual 'living' Ader who haunts the film's present is, in some ways, the most other-wordly image in the film, the least supported by any historical or material substance.

There is, again subtly but strikingly, a sense of intimacy and care in Robert's holding up of the cyclist that suggests this vulnerable body might be an object of desire. This effect is even more palpable in Robert's reframing of Ader's *Broken Fall (Organic)* (1971) where again he enters the scene from behind the camera to hold Ader who is this time hanging from a tree branch. Whereas in Ader's film the inevitable (and therefore, as Verwoert emphasises, quintessentially tragic) conclusion is the artist's fall from the tree into water below, here Robert lowers the hanging body gradually to safety, ending in an embrace that again shifts the affective tone away from the heroic/slapstick of Ader's films to something closer and more tender. It is not, I think, that Robert wishes this holding of 'Ader's' body to touch particularly on Ader or his work. Rather, the gesture makes for a deeply touching moment in the film, one in which the generalities of 'the body' in performance are recast in terms of the specificity of a loved body, the risks of leaving and being left located in terms of the bonds within relationships rather than the narrative arcs of tragedy.

POSING THE SUBJECT

A subsequent sequence of shots in *L'Education Sentimentale* continues this reworking and recoding of Ader's self-presentation but in a different register. We are shown, one after the other, two iconic 1970s record sleeves mounted on a wall, first that of Iggy Pop's 'The Idiot' (produced by David Bowie), then Bowie's own 'Heroes'. Next we see Robert standing between the two records, framed so that his legs and face are mostly cropped out. Robert mimics the poses pictured on each record, flowing between them and gradually incorporating other gestures in a performance that seems a mixture of the scripted and the casually spontaneous. The titles and cover art of these two records exemplify precisely the roles that Bas Jan Ader combined in his work – those of the artist as questing hero and as slapstick clown. Here Robert's gesturing body becomes the medium of their reconciliation. Furthermore, the fact that both musicians have derived their poses from a 1917 Expressionist portrait by Erich Heckel, and that this shared reference could be read as marking the closeness of their relationship, adds further layers to Robert's act of mediation. This section reinforces the inter-subjective poetics already seen in the previous sequences (adding to it a reference to icons of 70s culture from beyond the art world) but it also makes the issue of the pose a central one here.

In his essay 'Posing', Craig Owens focuses on a number of artistic practices that deploy the appropriation and staging of poses in relation to desire. Owens claims that, 'posing ... is a form of mimicry,' which he takes, following Lacan, to entail: 'a certain *splitting* of the subject: the entire body detaches itself from itself, becomes a picture, a semblance.'(12) Attention to this splitting through psychoanalytic, feminist and poststructuralist accounts of subjectivity, Owens contends, can reveal fault lines in the very constitution of normative subjectivity itself and show the complicity between images and power. Employing a Freudian model of fetishistic disavowal, Owens suggests that we find symptomatic 'fixated representations' emerging precisely at the points in culture where fundamental contradictions or impasses are located.[13] In the artworks that Owens discusses in this essay (including work by Victor Burgin, Barbara Kruger, Silvia Kolbowski and Sherrie Levine) critical mimicry is often directed against the putative originality, propriety, property status and representational authority of these symptomatically fetishistic images in our culture. The artistic task is taken to be the revealing and refusal of the imposture of such images, their claim to speak for or figure multiple subjectivities. Posing in critical art, then, is presented in Owens' essay as a mimicry of the stance of subjective mastery and of the illusory suspension or resolution of social contradictions. This mimicry reveals such mastery and such resolution to be nothing more than a pose.

As Jan Verwoert has again argued, the appropriation of images in art of the late 1970s and early 1980s often resulted in art works which took the form of still photographs, film stills, or of 'frozen images' (such as Robert Longo's drawings of falling men and women).[14] Owens reads this effect through the ambiguity of the French phrase *arrêt de mort* which, he notes: 'signifies both a death sentence and a stay of execution; the *arrêt* both condemns and grants reprieve, postpones the deciding of an antinomy.'[15] In a photographic image's freezing of an instant, Owens suggests, we have a characteristically 'fixated' fetishistic visual mode. He goes on to link this to Roland Barthes's famous account in *Camera Lucida* of the act of posing for the photograph as a similarly deathly freezing of time. Barthes gives the following account of his discomfort at being subjected to photography's arrest:

> *[O]nce I feel myself observed by the lens, everything changes: I constitute myself in the process of 'posing', I instantaneously make another body for myself, I transform myself in advance into an image. This transformation is an active one: I feel that the photograph creates my body or mortifies it, according to its caprice.*[16]

Barthes, to his chagrin, is unable to find a pose for himself that he feels matches his subjectivity, or conveys the depth of his feeling; instead the photographic portrait renders him an object, legible according to social codes, clichés or stereotypes of identity, but remote from his own sense of himself.

Might we then read Robert's work, which follows on from the kinds of critiques of representation that Owens and others pursued in the 1970s and 1980s, along these lines? After all, Robert deploys strategies of appropriation and posing pioneered in that period. In *L'Education Sentimentale* he arrests Ader's movement, preventing him from falling and thus 'stills' the image, and he employs posing as a form of mimicry, a copying of what is already a copy. Further, in the performance piece *Marriage à la Mode et Cor Anglais* (2009), Robert and his collaborator Ian White combine spoken passages from *Camera Lucida* including those which bemoan the mortifying process of posing for photographs – with a number of performed actions, amongst which was their own reposing of a Mapplethorpe photograph of Philip Glass and Robert Wilson. However, what seems to me an important difference between Robert's work and the practices theorised by Owens emerges precisely here, for Robert does not privilege either the mobility or the stillness of images, the presence or absence of bodies, the coding of the pose or the spontaneity of movement, but moves to and fro, back and forth across such oppositions. In operating in this way, the work gets closer to the double movement which is in fact at stake in both the content and the form of *Camera Lucida* itself, a movement that emerges from Barthes' sense of 'the uneasiness of being a subject torn between two languages, one expressive, the other critical.'(17) *Camera Lucida* continually slips between these languages, most pointedly once we enter the second part of Barthes's book and read of his intense grief for his mother, after whose death, he says, 'everything has remained motionless', and are told of his discovery of what becomes his prototype for all photography, the so-called 'Winter Garden Photograph' of his mother as a little girl.(18) Of this image, which he withholds from his readers on the grounds that it is traumatic, *real*, only for him and merely anecdotal for anyone else, Barthes stresses that he has nothing to say and that there is nothing he *can* say. Before this image, Barthes says: 'I am a bad dreamer who vainly holds out his arms toward the possession of the image.'(19) Here we might discern one of *Camera Lucida's* most salient features in the present context, namely the way it invokes a wish for tactile contact and for a language of affect, only to insist that these are beyond reach. This is the sentimental education which Barthes imparts.

The passage in which Barthes discusses the Mapplethorpe photograph that provides the first, still pose of *Marriage à la Mode...* is a good example here. It comes at the end of the first part of *Camera Lucida*, almost at the point where Barthes shifts markedly from the position of semiologist to that of inconsolable son. Having introduced his famous distinction between what is merely interesting, aesthetic, technical in a photograph (what he calls *stadium*) and what wounds, bruises or pricks (*punctum*), Barthes writes:

> *What I can name cannot really prick me. The incapacity to name is a good symptom of disturbance. Mapplethorpe has photographed Robert Wilson and Philip Glass. Wilson holds me, though I cannot say why, i.e., say where: is it the eyes, the skin, the position of the hands, the track shoes? The effect is certain but unlocatable, it does not find its sign, its name; it is sharp and yet lands in a vague zone of myself; it is acute yet muffled, it cries out in silence. Odd contradiction: a floating flash.*(20)

Camera Lucida is full of such odd contradictions, but *pace* Owens, it is not – or not only – Barthes' project to expose the photograph as fetishistically resolving them. Rather, again and again, it is these contradictory moments that the text actively engenders, against the claims of critique to see through them. Thus, past and present, life and death, real and represented are thoroughly entangled in the text and the distinctions Barthes does introduce continually break down. For example, having begun to build a distinction between film and photography on the grounds that only the former has a 'blind field' beyond the frame, Barthes returns to Mapplethorpe's photograph to undo that distinction: 'once there is a *punctum* a blind field is created (is divined),' so that 'Robert Wilson, endowed with an unlocatable *punctum*, is someone I want to meet.'(21) In his intimation of the desire an image might provoke, then, Barthes twice uses a language of touch: Wilson 'holds' him, he wants to contact Wilson. This language in fact pervades the book. Photography, Barthes argues, is not representation in the ordinary sense:

> *The photograph is literally an emanation of the referent. From a real body, which was there, proceed radiations which ultimately touch me, who am here; the duration of the transmission is insignificant... A sort of umbilical cord links the body of the photographed thing to my gaze: light, though impalpable, is here a carnal medium, a skin that I share with anyone who has been photographed.*(22)

In his searching analysis of *Camera Lucida*, Jay Prosser links Barthes' writing on photography to a longer tradition in which the photograph is treated as a second skin formed through loss.(23) For example, Prosser cites Nadar:

> *According to Balzac's theory, all physical bodies are made up entirely of layers of ghostlike images, an infinite number of leaflike skins laid one on top of the other. Since Balzac believed man was*

> *incapable of making something material from an apparition – that is, creating something from nothing – he concluded that every time someone had his photograph taken, one of the spectral layers was removed from the body and transferred to the photograph.*[24]

The photograph *is* the body of its referent, Balzac and Barthes contend. And yet, in the end, as the punctuating, puncturing Winter Garden Photograph reveals, even though Barthes won't show it to us, this holding on is a matter of loss of contact. The notion of a 'shared skin' put forward by Barthes brings to mind Didier Anzieu's concept of the 'common skin' phantasy, whereby a baby comes to conceive of their mother's skin as continuous with their own.[25] But the photograph, Barthes knows and laments, makes his mother's absence felt more keenly, it does not restore presence. As Brian Dillon notes, with *Camera Lucida*, 'Barthes had composed a ghost story of sorts, in which neither Henriette Barthes nor the book's ostensible subject, photography, could quite be grasped.'[26]

A concept of photography as a skin-like medium that we can touch, but which eludes our reach, is at the emotional heart of *Camera Lucida*, and it provides a useful point of reference in relation to Robert's solo performance piece, *Figure de Style* (2008). fig. 14 Filmed documentation of this performance reveals Robert's seemingly direct contact with an audience invited to take turns pulling away sections of masking tape which cover the artist's otherwise naked torso. Writing in *Frieze*, Kirsty Bell noted her surprise at discovering that pulling away the tape 'not only revealed the skin underneath, but also pulled it up to allow an intimate encounter with the artist's smooth brown skin – his own fragile surface.'[27] The sense of a contact with the skin taking place in the present tense of live performance is communicated only visually by the film document, so that the viewer is only too aware that they arrive too late to grasp the piece as it was originally staged. However, *Figure de Style* itself is structured so as to incorporate this belatedness and being out of touch into the performance itself. As the audience members took turns to approach Robert (thereby entering the camera frame which will ultimately make them part of the document of the work), he sporadically read from reviews of Yoko Ono's *Cut Piece* (first performed in Kyoto in 1964, and presented in London and New York the following year), after which his own work is clearly modelled.[28] Bell described how Robert's embodiment of Ono's pose combined with verbal traces of *Cut Piece's* reception created 'a palpable redoubling of the audience's self-consciousness: the words 'the audience squirmed uncomfortably', for instance, elicited an equivalent uncomfortable squirm. To be clear, in *Figure de Style* Robert does not attempt a return to the original moment of Ono's work, he does not restage or repeat *Cut Piece*, update or re-live it, but folds its problematic reception, its documentation in performance photographs and critical texts into the moment shared by Robert and the audience.

Not having touched Robert in the real time of the performance, only having watched others doing so on film, I can only defer to Bell's first hand account of what it felt like to be present and take part in it. As Hillis Miller has pointed out, the hand is implicit in the French word for 'now': *maintenant.*[31] All kinds of linguistic and philosophical traits link tactile contact to presence and to knowledge. And yet this work, and other films and performances by Robert including *L'Education Sentimentale*, seem to me to put the privilege of first hand experience in question, precisely by handling touch, like Barthes handles photography, as something that slips out of the present tense and is never fully present. The traces of the hand are felt frequently in Robert's work, and his use of images is often precisely a matter of handling: collages and works on paper might be folded, creased, scrunched, taped over, torn, and so on. In the 2007 work *Untitled (Belladonna)*, for instance, an inkjet print is smudged with charcoal that extends beyond its edges and creates an urgent whirl of handprints on the gallery wall. The effect is not so much to mark the work with an indexical 'I was here' or insist on the special place of the artist's own hand in the work, but rather to show how complex touch is, how difficult it is to put one's finger on. Is the gesture by which Robert effaces Bas Jan Ader's words to be understood in the same terms as his embrace of the stand-in for Ader? Is the touch of each audience member in *Figure de Style* tender or violent, a caress or a blow? When Robert projected a film onto his skin as part of the work *Counter-relief* (2007), could we say the film touched him? When we watch the document of *Figure de Style* does it touch us any less than those audience members?

The rhetoric of touch and being touched, and its deeply problematic place in the history of western thought, was the subject of one of Jacques Derrida's most dense and most provocative late texts, *On Touching – Jean-Luc Nancy* (2005). In unpicking what philosophy has tried to say about touch, Derrida plays incessantly with figures of speech indebted to touch, tact, tangents, contingency, and so on. The excessive recourse to such turns of phrase in the present essay is only a muted echo of Derrida's. The problem at the heart of the book is how Derrida can touch another thinker, Jean-Luc Nancy, who is himself preoccupied with touch. To touch Nancy would be both to move him and to take him in hand, to get to grips with his work. But Derrida will be concerned to show that touching or moving another subject does not evade language or move directly to their heart. Miller describes the crucial thematic of *On Touching* as:

> *the untouchability at the heart of touch, the impossibility both of touching itself and of talking/writing directly about touch. You cannot touch touch, or touch on touch. An interval, interruption, or spacing that cannot itself be touched, any more than can the object of touch or the limit of touch, always intervenes between my finger and what I reach out to touch...*[32]

By reading Nancy, and a tradition stretching back to Aristotle, on touch and its relation to knowledge and to other senses, Miller contends,

> *Derrida wants to show that all [...] (1) there is no 'the' touch; and (2) the commonsense intuition of an immediacy and intimacy of touch never happens, not even when I touch myself touching myself. Touch is always mediated, distanced, divided, parted, translated, grafted, prosthetic, like Nancy's transplanted heart, a constant theme or figure, theme/figure, in Le Toucher.*[33]

How to reach another, how to move another, how to say the unsayable, how to think touch without immediacy, as syncopated rather than synchronized: these are among the questions with which Derrida wrestles, and which make his writing relevant to Robert's work.

In the final scene of *L'Education Sentimentale*, we see a reproduction of Bas Jan Ader's *I'm Too Sad to Tell You* stuck to the wall (as images so often are in artists' studios). Robert's hand reaches into the frame and, scrunching it up, pulls it from the wall. The gesture is deeply ambivalent. It might signal artistic independence from such precursors (the title of Robert's work, after all, is borrowed from a coming-of-age story), it could suggest a refusal of melancholic holding on, a moving on from Ader's inexpressible sadness, or – closer to Barthes – a frustration with any image that codes emotion. As at the beginning of the film, the artist's hand takes away as well as makes or gives, and throughout *L'Education Sentimentale*, 'touch,' as Derrida insists in *On Touching...*, is not one thing, but many: by turns a caress, a blow, an erasure.

Derrida borrows the phrase 'exscription' to name the inevitability (in touching on what touches) that whatever one might say is: 'written away or effaced, on the skin, that is, at the untouchable limit of what you are trying to touch.'(34) This might well figure the mingling of skin, touch, affect and language that Robert's work presents. *L'Education Sentimentale*, like much of Robert's art, moves gracefully but urgently back and forth between what can and cannot be said, what can and cannot be touched upon, between the tactile and the visual, and between the present and the past.

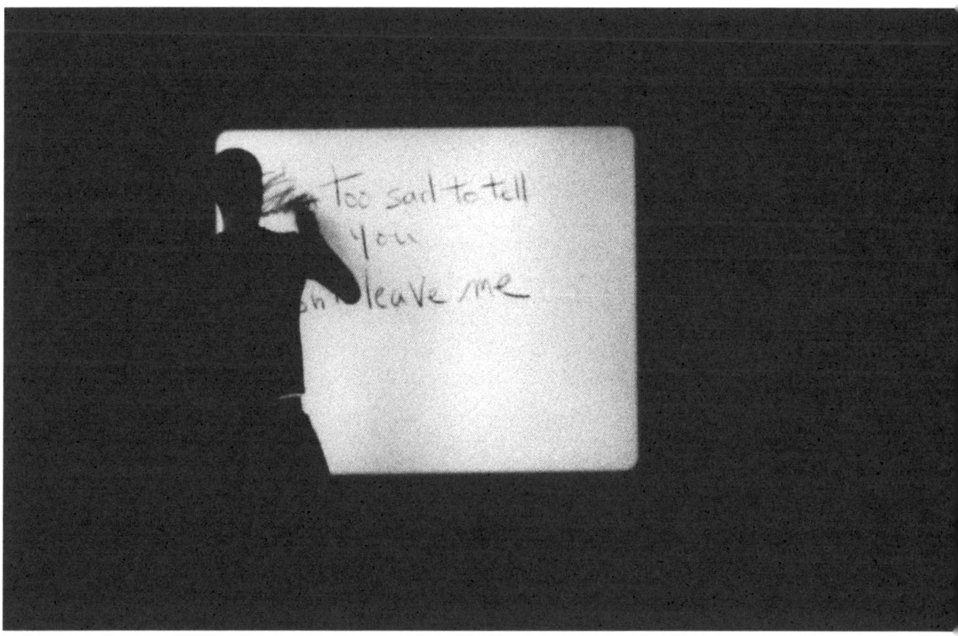

Jimmy Robert, *L'Education Sentimentale* (2005): 35mm film still.

ENDNOTES

(1) Roland Barthes, *Mourning Diary*, trans. Richard Howard (New York: Hill and Wang, 2010), p. 168.

(2) Jacques Derrida, *On Touching - Jean-Luc Nancy*, trans. Christine Irizarry (Stanford: Stanford University Press, 2005), p. 293.

(3) 'Expand images, materialize reading, live in language: An Interview with Jimmy Robert by Vanessa Desclaux,' http://www.zerodeux.fr/entretien-avec-jimmy-robert-par-vanessa-desclaux Last accessed 11/8/2011.

(4) Robert has noted that part of the impetus for referring to Ader's work came from the coincidental fact that at the time of making *L'Education Sentimentale* he was studying at the Rijksakademie in Amsterdam nearly 30 years after Ader's disappearance. Correspondence with the author, May 2010.

(5) A later work, *Thoughts Unsaid, Then Forgotten* (1973) reprised the presentational format of *Please Don't Leave Me,* with the addition of a vase of flowers. Here Ader included the instruction that the exhibiting gallery paint over and obliterate the titular text after a few days, leaving the other elements in place - a strategy evoked subtly in Robert's actions in *L'Education Sentimentale.*

(6) On the pose of melancholy in relation to art history see Keith Moxey, 'Panofsky's Melancolia,' in *The Practice of Theory: Poststructuralism, Cultural Politics, and Art History* (Ithaca: Cornell University Press, 1994), pp. 65-78.

(7) Alexandra Blättler and Rein Wolfs, 'The Works of *Bas Jan Ader,' in Bas Jan Ader: Please Don't Leave Me*, ed. Rein Wolfs (Rotterdam: Museum Boijmans van Beuningen, 2006), p. 78

(8) Jan Verwoert, *Bas Jan Ader: In Search of the Miraculous* (London: Afterall, 2006), p. 20.

(9) *Ibid.*, p. 42.
We might note that a further distinction undone in *I'm Too Sad to Tell You* is that between the 'original' performance and the film as mere mediating document - here, the performance itself is shown to be always already mediated.

(10) The struggle Robert presents between inscription and erasure, and between self and other (within the self) suggest a resonance here with Hegel's famous account of the subject's struggle for recognition and the emergence of the 'unhappy consciousness'.

(11) See Jorg Heiser, 'Curb your romanticism: Bas Jan Ader's slapstick,' in *Bas Jan Ader: Please Don't Leave Me*, ed. Rein Wolfs, pp. 25-28.

(12) Craig Owens, 'Posing,' *Beyond Recognition: Representation, Power, and Culture* (London: University of California Press, 1994), p. 212.

(13) *Ibid.* p. 210.

(14) Jan Verwoert, 'Living with Ghosts: From Appropriation to Invocation,' in *Tell Me What You Want, What You Really, Really Want*, ed. Vanessa Ohlraun (Berlin: Sternberg, 2010), pp.127-148.

(15) Craig Owens, 'Posing,' *Beyond Recognition: Representation, Power, and Culture*, p. 210.

(16) Roland Barthes, *Camera Lucida: Reflection on Photography*, trans. Richard Howard (London: Vintage, 2000), pp. 10, 11.

(17) *Ibid.* p. 8.

(18) *Ibid.* p. 75.

(19) *Ibid.* p. 100.

(20 *Ibid.* p. 51, 53.

(21) *Ibid.* p. 55.

(22) *Ibid.* p. 80, 81.

(23) Jay Prosser, *Light in the Dark Room: Photography and Loss* (Minneapolis: University of Minnesota Press, 2005), pp. 179-181.

(24) Nadar, 'My Life as a Photographer,' trans. Thomas Repensek, October, Vol. 5, 1978, p. 9.

(25) See Naomi Segal, *Consensuality: Didier Anzieu, Gender and the Sense of Touch* (New York: Rodopi, 2009), pp. 31-53.

(26) Brian Dillon, 'Re-reading: *Camera Lucida* by Roland Barthes,' The Guardian, Saturday 26th March, 2011, p. 20.

(27) Kirsty Bell, 'Jimmy Robert,' *Frieze*, No. 115, May, 2008, http://www.frieze.com/issue/article/jimmy_robert/ Last accessed 2/3/12.

(28) The multiple instantiations of Ono's piece and the shifting meanings attributed to it are insightfully considered in Julia Bryan-Wilson, 'Remembering Yoko Ono's *Cut Piece,*' *Oxford Art Journal*, Vol. 26, No. 1, 2003, pp. 99-123, and in Kevin Concannon, 'Yoko Ono's Cut Piece: From Text to Performance and Back Again,' *PAJ: A Journal of Performance and Art*, Vol. 30, No. 3, September 2008, pp. 81-93.

(29) Peggy Phelan, *Unmarked: The Politics of Performance* (London: Routledge, 2005), p. 146.

(30) Amelia Jones, '"Presence" in Absentia: Experiencing Performance as Documentation,' *Art Journal*, Vol. 56, No. 4, Winter, 1997, p. 12.

(31) J. Hillis Miller, *For Derrida* (New York: Fordham, 2009), p. 249.

(32) Ibid, p. 273

(33) Ibid, p. 278

(34) J. Hillis Miller, 'Touching Derrida Touching Nancy: The Main Traits of Derrida's Hand,' *Derrida Today*, Vol. 1, No. 2, p. 148.

Between the Body and Object the Voice Appears: Yael Davids' *Learning to Imitate* and *Learning to Imitate in Absentia*

LISA PANTING

Between the body and object the voice appears.

Bridging the space between objects – simultaneously props, maybe even sculptures. Perhaps it is their status in tension with the performance that enlivens them – *part* object, prop or sculpture dependent on the forms of address moving through them – an action, a quotation and a recitation. Yael Davids' *Learning to Imitate* (2010) and *Learning to Imitate in Absentia* (2011) propose a manifold relationship to time and space. The before and after of the space – that is the temporality that moves with and through these mis-en-scènes – enables the works to mediate both installation and performance. Coalescing in the space between art and theatre these performances operate through a series of slippages of signs and systems. A syntax to be both explored and to decode.

Learning to Imitate is a performance work lasting 40 minutes. Davids moves around an installation with specific choreographed movements – from up high, hanging on a rope to the lowness of rolling down a staircase-like prop. The work is physical. She is dressed in a plain utilitarian looking Physical Education kit. *Learning to Imitate* explores the history of the voice – the way that the power of the voice is embedded in the fabric of our understanding – from speech acts, to singing, to the limits expressed by animals in the throws of death. These references traverse mythology to the voice in film and then theatre. Davids recites:

> *A similar conviction can be found in psychotherapy, a system based on speech. Lacan was interested in the expression of truth,*

> *of 'becoming' during speech. Voice is the first expression, it comes prior to self-identification in the mirror. In psychoanalysis, descriptions of the voice come prior to those of the gaze.*
>
> __ Learning to Imitate in Absentia

This 'becoming' is a valuable trope for the work, whilst also limiting. As we watch the artist we follow her memorised words. They stumble, we struggle with them – a bond and discord is created in this moment. She says:

> *When the voice gets re-attached to the body its aura crumbles, it loses its supreme character and becomes human again.*
>
> __ Learning to Imitate in Absentia

And we struggle with this becoming human for most of the performance, the in and out of the body – the creation of different time zones through oral image making – while being brought back into the present again. The audience hears the story, aligns the objects with an idea that is immediate but which also brings to the fore questions of construction versus authenticity, looking versus hearing. The performance is bound by a dialectical approach – the subject to the object, the voice and the gaze. The dialectic is connected to the physical realities of the body – the struggle is everything within this reality – and the question is how to construct an experience that destabilizes our perception of that reality. An understanding of this performance identifies the text as a series of reflections that come into view: researched fragments, written text and quotes that build a narrative between the voice, the body and the object. Davids' subject position is a destabalising force; where her narrative approach asks how we build history, how the contingency of the body presides over the course of events – where the 'aura' of the voice can only be temporary and contingent, fading from view.

The vicissitudes of memory.

The immediacy of the voice.

Leaning to Imitate II was performed at Picture This as part of a tour. The space is raw, with acoustic problems not previously faced by the artist in the Frascati Theater, Amsterdam or the museum space of Van Abbemuseum, Eindhoven. A physical challenge was presented. The work is about the voice, but the voice could not easily be heard. This was a paradox that made the work hard for the space. But the artist wanted to work with this problem, the unfriendliness of space – its harshness. To protect the voice, Davids proposed using large-scale acoustic boards, that would in theory uphold the voice, and, with the involvement of participants, be choreographed to move around the space according to her positioning. The boards were of different sizes. One massive board needed a group of eight people to move with it. Others were like body-sized shields. Reminiscent of both the scene in Shakespeare's *Macbeth* where the forest starts to move (here the walls started to move), and a post-minimalist ballet, we don't know if the material aided the resonance of Davids' voice but the resulting effect was an orchestration that set the entire space in motion. This 'image' created a push and pull of scale, between the meta, the mega and littleness – a tableau vivant encoding historical and conceptual modes of signification.

As Anthony Vidler has noted: 'Modernity has been haunted, as we know very well, by a myth of transparency: transparency of the self to nature, of the self to the other, of all selves to society, and all this represented, if not constructed...'. [1] The movement of the boards in combination with the texts animated this relationship and clearly fed into the next iteration of the work at Picture This the following year where transparency became manifest through the materiality of the piece, which in this instance used glass. Glass mediates the obscure to the transparent. Its history of production captures the construction of both ancient and modern worlds. It both supports and evades reflection. Lacan links the moment of identification of the self to the reflection of the self. To know it's you, to identify the voice as coming from *your* body. However, unlike the Lacan, Davids never uses the mirror: the reflections produced by the glass sheets are more obscured, less stable images that create a spatial effect with only *partial* potential for identification – fragmentary images where the body of Davids, and equally, the bodies of you or of me, fold in and out of view. An elegiac sensibility infused Davids' process in this way – underpinned by the nature of the actual space which had since been painted black – but also by a recent loss in the artist's own life. A *notion* of grief and an actual *experience* gave momentum to this manifestation. Revisiting *Learning to Imitate* as a score for a new performance, *Learning to Imitate in Absentia* experimented with the *emptiness* that appears *after* a performance. A central question addressed by the work is how grief can manifest itself in art. Davids wants to look at performance, which by its very nature carries an element of loss – by the nature of its temporality, it progresses towards its own end.

fig. 16

At Picture This, we wanted to take an exploratory approach to working with an artist, with minimal reference to the moving image in actual terms, but conceptually engaged with notions of representation and repetition in more open dialogue with the idea of 'staging'– paradigms locked into current questions of making some contemporary film and video art. Looking outside of the conceptual tropes of experimental video and film, theatre and filmic conventions interest artists wishing to move away from the 'immediacy' of the camera. This creates controlled, constructed situations to search out ways that question notions of address, structures of power and the mediated image within a context of image saturation (at Picture This – Rachel Ruepke, Maryam Jafri and Hito Steyerl explored these questions in some form). Davids' work presented a counterpoint to the boundaries imposed by the frame, bringing a more discursive form of address into play. It held significance to invite an artist to make work at Picture This who asked different things of us, where dialogue and negotiation informed the process, shifting between *Learning to Imitate* in 2010 and *Learning to Imitate in Absentia* the following year. Being integrated into the production process – spatially, technically and conceptually brings different knowledge, other insights – once bound to the space, echoes bound back and resurface.

In Davids' second appearance at Picture This, acoustic boards became replaced by statically arranged sheets of glass – the earlier performance with a group of participants became a solo act and the inflection more self-reflexive. Here she begun by asking:

> *As I come to terms with the end of one performance and its residuum in space, in things and in me, I wonder if the idea of documentation and notation came about to enable the restaging and celebration of dance or performance? Or rather as an expression of a constant searching for the ones who move, the ones who erase, and the ones who undo themselves.*
>
> — *Learning to Imitate*

Three points of movement that extend back, forward and into, moving literally, moving metaphorically.

The glasshouse effect of the installation became reminiscent of the transparency that Vidler identifies as a paradigm of modernism. To live in a glasshouse, was according to Walter Benjamin an 'intoxication, a moral exhibitionism that we badly need'.(2) For Davids, glass and transparency are more fraught then that. Materially, the glass may offer transparency, here glass is used as a mechanism to work with the black of the space creating alternative fields of vision.

However, when in the hands of Oran Safety Glass, a company based in the Kibbutz Tzuba where Davids was born, the production of window glass evolved through differing production demands into the production of bullet proof glass – resistant to machine gun fire and soon even to RPG (rocket propelled grenades) and bazooka grenades. A sample of this glass sat on the floor. It's a brick of glass that transcends understanding – an unfamiliar object, whilst being wholly familiar, a complicated object both repellant and beautiful. So much of the history of materials has become embedded within art history but this sample cannot be recouped so easily into the discourse of art. The smallest object in the room but the most challenging – a *punctum* that ruptured a straightforward assimilation of the work, depositing a sense of conflict.

Conflict – about the role of materials and its relationship to art practice.

Conflict – between the political realities of Israel.

Conflict – that Davids expresses and draws upon.

Conflict – between what we know and how we feel.

Zvad- zvat
Tveriya- tveira
Bisan- Beit Shean
A-Nazra - nazerat
Yafa- Yafo
Ramle- Ramle
El Kads- Jerushaleyim
Br Al Sabha- Beer Seva
Zuba- Tzuba

I grew up in Kibbutz Tzuba - down hill. Up hill were the beautiful ruins of an old Arab village Zuba. We called it 'The Arab Tzuba', we loved walking there as kids – a beautiful location with a beautiful view.

(showing photos of the ruins of Zuba)

> *Years later I learned that what we have been told about the history of these ruins was not that innocent. Zuba has been a Palestinian village that was attacked in 13 July 1948 by The Palmach army. The 602 Palestinian villagers were expelled, and a Zionistic settlement Kibbutz Tzuba was established on the land of this village. My growing up was somewhere between these two places Zuba and Tzuba, somewhere between these two mental spaces.*
>
> __ *Learning to Imitate in Absentia*

To learn to imitate is to memorise.

In these works, Davids learns her lines, sometimes pulling forth a crumpled note to read a quotation. The act is full of stuttering, restarts and she closes her eyes – creating a private space. We witness this private act – like all performance, it carries with it the risk of failed memory, forgotten words. The invitation to become part of this as audience, to traverse this mental space isn't always easy. Davids' *modus operandi* isn't theatre, as that emphasis would be too instructive for the artist because it would imply a closed circuit, a direct address. Like all performances, it identifies itself in tension with theatre and for Davids also dance. The voice, its projection perhaps the most 'auratic' element of *Learning to Imitate*, and *Learning to Imitate in Absentia* is in the end the element that traverses these different forms, that pulls you into the 'performed' space – but where the installation elements flex their relationship, never recreating the hierarchy between prop and performer, pushing and pulling to destabilise 'theatre' enough to create a relationship to it, without *being* it. Davids' circuit is more open, and error, failure and repetition are constitutive of the space created. As much as history is fraught, the *now* is complex – and the subject is one that, for Davids' performance work at least, is always in a state of becoming.

ENDNOTES

(1) Anthony Vidler, *The Architectural Uncanny* (Cambridge, Massachusetts and London: MIT Press, 1994), p. 217.

(2) Walter Benjamin, 'Surrealism', in *Selected Writings Vol. 2* (Harvard University Press, 2003), p. 209.

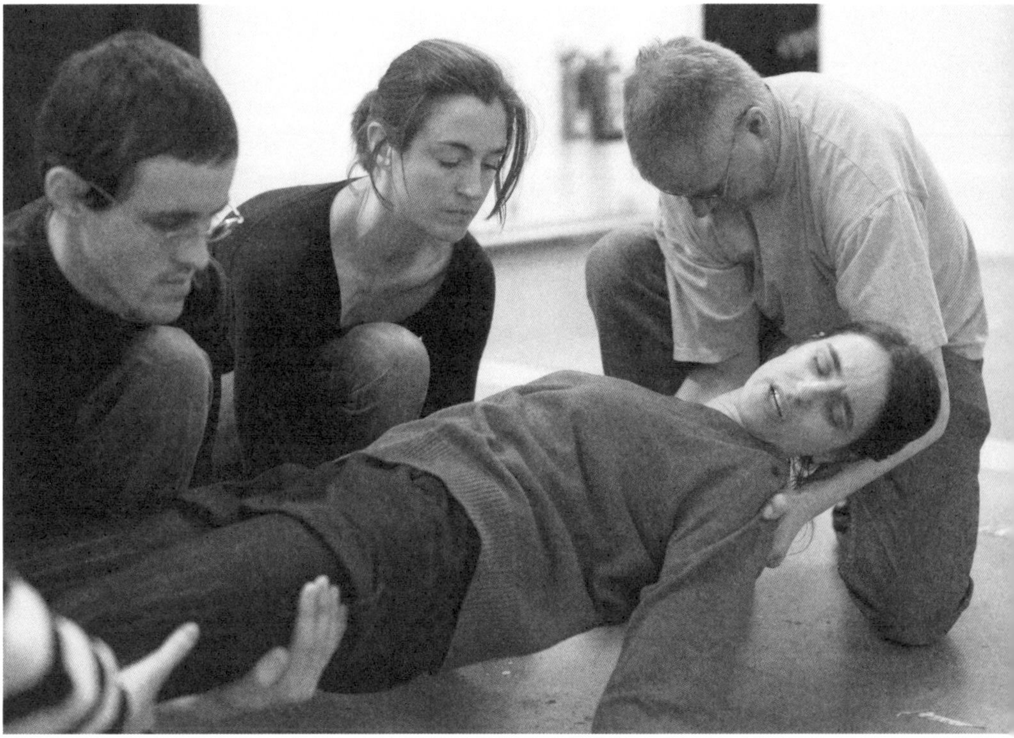

Yael Davids, *Learning to Imitate* (2010): performance documentation, Picture This.
Photo: Max McClure.

The Subject in Process: Material Equations in the Work of Carolee Schneemann and Annabel Nicolson

LUCY REYNOLDS

It was during the editing of her film *Fuses* (1963), Carolee Schneemann recalls that she began to consider how shared formal properties, or a 'material equation,' could be made between film and performance:

> *Until that time I'd considered filmmaking only as an independent, discrete, self-contained language. But studying the film as it was split into multiple moving images and planes shifted my reticence about including film in performance.* Fuses *was structured to emphasise my concern with impacting and intensifying the focal plane, the illusory spatial dimensions – while at the same time 'breaking' the frame by scratching, dying, bleaching, cutting and gluing frames, layering and collage. Because of its visual complexity a film such as* Fuses *couldn't become part of a performance. But I saw the way film could be activated by literal, formal properties into a material equation with the constructions: increasing the ambiguity of the focal plane of film into actual space; extending, compounding repetitions and variations of color, texture and literal imagery from film into environment and performance.*[1]

When she devised *Ghost Rev* (1965), her first fusion of performance and film, Schneemann had already developed a creative practice in which her own body played a central role of overt self-expression across a range of mediums, becoming a potent space through which to confront and explode the conflicted questions of gender and sexuality that were circulating in the moral climate of the post-war period. Her single screen film *Fuses* (1963-67), for example, explicitly depicts the lovemaking between herself and her partner the composer James Tenney; and *Meatjoy* (1964), comprising eight

naked performers including herself who interacted with a variety of different materials, including meat and fish, in order to evoke: 'the character of an erotic rite: excessive, indulgent, a celebration of
fig. 17 flesh as material.' (2) Later, in *Snows* (1969) and *Illinois Central* (1968), the naked body of the performer became part of ambitious 'kinetic theatre' events which used film projection, kinetic devices and especially composed scores to address her political opposition to the war in Vietnam.

The overt presentation of the body in Schneemann's work could be seen as part of the wider tendency that occurred in the 1960s towards a more temporally inflected art practice that sought to break down the distinctions between art forms, where the live event and the artist's body became a convergence point at which different media, including film, could coalesce. The body's new agency cannot be separated from the political ferment of the period: in the increasingly active multi-stranded forms of protest against American involvement in Vietnam and the nuclear threat, and in the challenges to gender and racial discrimination raised by the women's liberation and the black power movement. In this radicalised context, the body takes on a new significance as an instrument of dissent, asserting a collective oppositional presence at protest rallies, 'sit-ins' and on marches. Individually, it serves as a site of advocacy for the liberalised counter-cultural lifestyle of the period, in which, as Schneemann's practice shows, the overt display of the body as a sexually enlightened subject directly challenges societal codes of morality.

It is perhaps not surprising then, as John Sayre reflects, that: '[P]erformance was quickly hit upon as one of the better strategies for making art in such overtly politicized times.' (3) The body's oppositional role in political protest was extended into an oppositional space in culture that challenged the art establishment of the day, whose institutions, and the prevailing theories of Greenbergian modernism they upheld, were seen as complicit with the dominant political system. Emerging from these determining contexts, Schneemann's use of her own body might thus be understood as opening up a differentiated dialogue with her audience beyond the detached perspective proscribed for the modernist viewer. The feminist art theorist Amelia Jones, for example, proposes that the diverse and complex subjectivities of body artists such as Schneemann challenge and break down the hegemony and authority of the modernist practice and critique that was still current in the visual arts at the end of the 60s. For Jones the performance work of Schneemann and others challenged the orthodoxies of modernism by rethinking the body through performance, as contingent to the contexts of time, space and their own subjectivity, and: 'always particularized rather than universal, implicating the interpreter (with all her investedness, biases and desires) within the meanings and cultural values ascribed to the work of art.'(4) In this way their performances can be seen to anticipate or act, according to Jones, as a 'hinge' between modernism and post-modernism, offering an 'intersubjectivity' based on Merleau Ponty's phenomenological model, that recognises the significance of the mutual exchange between the performer and the spectator, both affecting the other.

Narrative Cinema, like the codes and conventions of modernism, also calls for a detached viewer who is distanced from their own live experience of the film projection as the action on-screen draws them into a time and space of fictional dimensions, a situation which is intensified by the darkened unobtrusive conditions of the cinema auditorium: a 'closed space' according to Jean Michel Baudry, where those who remain there 'find themselves chained, captured, or captivated.'(5) In works such as Schneemann's *Snows*, the interplay of film projection and the performing body breaks this spell and demands a dialogue of reciprocation between viewer and performer. As Schneemann contended:

> *I wanted to use film as integral to performance while emphasizing it as a contrasting visual language – handled as tactile, palpable material... I didn't want to insert film as subordinate image concentrations: nor did I want image juxtapositions apart from the overall spatial texture. Each element (movement film, lights, sound) was created to hold its defining edge and to merge with surrounding units.'* (6)

Presented at the Martinique Theater in New York as part of 'Angry Arts Week', *Snows* made visceral use of Schneemann's film *Viet Flakes* (1965), which was constructed from reportage footage of the war and projected in disquieting contrast alongside 'silent reels of ruddy Bavarians at play' – 1930s films of Bavarian skiing resorts that Schneemann had found.(7) With the help of the inter-media organisation Experiments in Art and Technology she was able to realise a complex audio visual show in which the films were projected on a 360 degree axis across a 'revolving light sculpture'– a rotating white disc at the back of the stage. Meanwhile, accompanied by a score composed by James Tenney, a group of performers improvised 'body sculptures' in response to the films projected over them.

Opening up the film event as an experience of flux and indeterminacy, the performers on stage thus activated an embodied yet ambiguous space between stage and screen image. The patina of film projections cast over their bodies functioned as a form of camouflage or concealment, enfolding the performers into the film image; whilst at the same time the contingency of their improvised real-time movements breaks through this homogeneity, to insert an unpredictable element of live presence into the viewer's experience of the film. This was compounded by the audience's direct and unwitting participation in *Snows*, for the pattern of their own sounds and movements were relayed from contact mikes under their seats to the performers on stage as a series of visual cues.[8] Schneemann's own remembrance gives a compelling sense of the overall effect: 'The structural intervals and gradations of light and darkness, the paper-layered walls, the water lenses and revolving light sculpture, the performance movement, the highly visible technicians: each element was drawn into a vortex of disturbing energy.'[9]

This merging between immaterial surfaces and human corporality calls to mind the concept of haptic perception or visuality first developed by the 19th century art historian Alois Riegl[10] and more recently elaborated by Laura Marks in relation to film, where 'the eyes themselves function like organs of touch,' eliciting a viewing experience that: 'tends to move over the surface of its object rather than plunge into illusionistic depth, not to distinguish form so much as to discern texture.'[11] Marks suggests that this tactile experience of cinema as surface forces the viewer: 'to contemplate the image itself instead of being pulled into narrative.'[12]

It could be argued that the haptic exchange between the bodies of film, performer and viewer in works such as *Snows* thus proposes a different form of spectatorship both for cinema and for the visual arts. Schneemann's inter-position of the performing body reasserted film as a live experience occurring in the space of the spectator, no longer in thrall to narrative strictures of time and space on the screen but beholden to a spread of surface and movement. At the same time, returning to notions of the intersubjective, the performer's corporeal presence demands a dialogical engagement with the viewer: a time and space of embodiment where the performance of one is met in the performance of the other, in a mode of participation which exceeds the bounds of the cinema screen and the conventions of detachment required by modernism. In the case of *Snows* whose film images depicted the maimed and wounded victims of Vietnam, these processes of reciprocal embodiment brought the war closer to the viewer, with a sense of corporeal reality and visceral power.

However, a third dialogue exists beyond the intersubjective reciprocities between spectator, artist and film image noted by Jones or Marks: that of the artist's own dialogue with their materials. In the case of Schneemann this might equally be the matter of paint as well as celluloid and projected light, always in relationship to the surfaces of her own body. As such, Schneemannn insists, as David Levi Strauss asserts: 'on the physicality of all her artmaking,' by literally painting herself into her work in early pieces such as *Eye Body* (1963), for example.(13) We might understand Schneemann's approach as indicative of a tactile identification with her materials, where the 'material equation' between the film's immaterial projections and her own corporeal presence unfolds before the audience as an intimate process of personal exploration.

Here Jones' notion of intersubjectivity between performer and audience becomes extended into what I call the *subject-in-process*, in which Schneemann's creative enquiry becomes performance as she unfolds her questioning relationship with her materials into the context of the live event. At the same time, through this intimate engagement with her materials, Schneemann becomes enfolded within them, part of a haptic reciprocity between her own body and the medium she is exploring. In *Snows* the performer is caught on the threshold between this interplay of material and immateriality as a *body-becoming-film-becoming-body*, viscerally merging with the damaged bodies of the Vietnamese projected upon them.

There is, however, a further body discernible in Schneemann's haptic exchange: that of the technological apparatus of film itself. Whilst Schneemann's discussion of her material equations with film does not refer directly to the projection apparatus, focusing instead on the frames of the film strip, its importance is clear in practice: seen both in her multiple use of projectors in *Snows*, which are highly visible at the edge of the stage, and the confidence with which she mixed different mechanical devices to create her effects during the event.

Schneemann was not alone in her attempts to bring the technology behind the effects of cinema into the light and to the attention of the viewer. To give two diverse examples: the 'expanded cinema' pioneer Stan Vanderbeek had also made his banks of projectors highly visible and audible as they transmitted an 'image-flow' of film projections into the circular space of his Moviedrome in 1966, and in his 1967 performance *Schnitte Fur ABABA* the German artist Werner Nekes closed the distances between the projector, the audience and his own body by carrying the projector close to his body in the manner of a camera, projecting it across the surfaces of the bodies and the gallery interior caught in his improvised path. By drawing attention to the projector as another performing body alongside their own, artists such as these, involved with expanded cinema practices of the 60s and early 70s, thus asserted the live and dynamic aspect of film projection. In this way, it could be argued, they re-imagined cinema as an art practice: to be experienced like a performance or a happening.

One of the most celebrated and intriguing examples of an artist's dialogue with her apparatus exists in Annabel Nicolson's film performance *Reel Time* (1973). Performed at several different events following its first presentation at the London Filmmakers' Co-op in May 1973, the artist was seated at a sewing machine in the centre of the space, and passed a film-strip, depicting an image of herself sewing, under the puncturing needle of the sewing machine and back through the projector in an continuous loop that was only broken when the destroyed film strip became too fragile to pass through the gate. The incremental destruction of Nicolson's image on the filmstrip, as it passed under the needle of the sewing machine, was experienced as a gradually disintegrating on-screen image, set in stark contrast to a juxtaposed silhouette of the artist, cast from the constant light of an adjacent projector. Concurrently, in the light available from the projections, two readers recited snatches of instruction for threading a sewing machine and threading a projector. The performance ended when the film-strip finally splintered under the destruction wrought by Nicolson's needle and was unable to be projected.

The palpable entropy of *Reel Time* has, until recently, been read through the common cause which Nicolson shared with many of her Co-op colleagues, whose purpose, like that of Schneemann, Vanderbeek or Nekes, was to elicit an activated and participatory form of cinema spectatorship in the viewer, and to achieve this by making visible the tools of cinema production, normally hidden in the edit room, film lab or projection booth. *Reel Time's* emphasis on the experience of the film projection as a live event reflected Malcolm Le Grice's articulations of a newly activated experience of spectatorial time and space in his influential essay, 'Real TIME/SPACE,' in which he stresses the importance of the projection process rather than the on-screen narrative as the 'current, tangible point of access for the audience', which would make the viewer alert to the experience of cinema as a live event, unfolding around them.[14]

To understand the context for Le Grice's position it is important to situate him in the wider ethos of the Co-op at this time, where the artisanal practices of the artist, supported by the readily available printing and processing equipment there, converged with a politically motivated rejection of the modes and practices of 'dominant' narrative cinema to create a unique and radical dialectic, where politics were inscribed into the processes and practices of the film medium. The multiple screens, 'film actions' and live event structures of expanded cinema works revealed to the viewer the disjuncture between the prefilmed 'retrospective reality' of the image on-screen, and – in an echo of Jones' particularised performing body – the contingent experience of 'real time/space' specific to the spatial and temporal conditions of the live performed event. For a short period between 1970 and 1974, expanded film action events such as Nicolson's *Reel Time* or Le Grice's suggestive shadow play performance, *Horror Film 1* (1970) flourished in a number of venues such as Gallery House, the ICA and the Walker Art Gallery in Liverpool. The mobile audiences and more flexible temporal and spatial conditions of gallery spaces such as these, offered new ways for British filmmakers to explore film as a live event and were often used as improvised workshop spaces to develop ideas about the 'primacy of the projection event' in concert with a participating audience.[15]

But whilst the British expanded practitioners of the period such as Nicolson used performance as part of a strategy to reveal illusionism and undermine modes of cinematic representation, at the same time performance and the body introduced an unavoidable subjectivity to their work; this allowed the intrusion of a representative element which would seem to challenge the wider rejection of narrative cinema in which they were engaged. For it could be argued that the process-led, systematic approach of Co-op filmmakers was equally as rooted in the detached critiques of modernism as other areas of the visual arts. Furthermore, could the strategies of intersubjective exchange between viewer and performer by which artists such as Schneemann, as Jones argues, sought to undo this alienated mode of engagement, be detected in the work of artists such as Nicolson or Le Grice, who seemed more interested in understanding the identity of the film apparatus than their own?

The answer lies in a differently nuanced reading of intersubjectivity than in the example of Schneemann's haptic enfoldment into the film projections of *Snows*. For in *Reel Time*, Nicolson's subjectivity is less a material equation than a dispersal of her own subjective presence across the bodies of the technology and apparatus that she explores: submerged and resurfacing through the technology as different evocations of self – onscreen, performing at her sewing machine and also an adjacent shadow self, literally 'shadowing' her dissolving film image. In addition, the systematic destruction of her own on-screen image under the needle of the sewing machine evokes a host of interpretations, prompting Le Grice's definition that it 'challenges quite basic assumptions about entropy – the loss of information through dispersal or "noise,"' (16) to my own explorations of a feminist confrontation of her own on-screen objectification, through Laura Mulvey's Lacanian inflected theories of the 'male gaze.' (17)

Furthermore, both pieces of apparatus were invested with subjective significance for Nicolson, the sewing machine served as a touchstone, a signifier of herself rather than more generalised female labour.(18) She did not consciously recognise the machine's gender connotations, as an instrument of female domestic labour, but associated it directly to her sense of herself as an artist: the sewing machine was kept in her studio and was 'part of my environment.' (19) She felt equally connected to the projector, seeing that aspect of the filmmaking process as the part she was most drawn to for its play of light and shadow. Indeed, the very obsolescence of Nicolson's apparatus, old models which had now been superseded by more modern machines, harked back to an earlier, and more explicitly artisanal, filmmaking practice, which, like shadow play, evoked a pre-narrative film period with which she and her fellow formalist filmmakers could identify.(20)

In this way, Nicolson invests her outdated equipment with some measure of the aura that Walter Benjamin noted as latent in the scratched surfaces of the discarded and outmoded art and objects of the pre-industrial era. For Benjamin this perception of the object's auratic power could be drawn forth by the reciprocated gaze between object and beholder, where: '[T]o perceive the aura of an object we look at means to invest it with the ability to look at us in return.'(21) His prescient intimations of the tactile exchanges of haptic perception can be identified in Nicolson's subjective engagement with the personal and historical narratives already inscribed in the shapes and worn surfaces of the projector and the sewing machine, playing another important part of her dialogue with the materials which structured her creative practice.

Thus, both artists use their bodies, through the act of performance, as a mode of enquiry not only to open up a new and dynamic mode of cinema to the viewer, but also to reach for a more intimate understanding of their own relationship to film. The counter-cultural context of happenings and performance in late 60s New York in which Schneemann realised *Snows* may present a strong contrast to the political and creative conditions of the London in which Nicolson later devised *Reel Time*. However, despite their differences of approach, *Snows* and *Reel Time* show how, as *the subject in process*, Schneemann and Nicolson's own identities become inseparable from their tactile and performative questioning of film's material and technological nature. Whether that may be through the haptic merging between the body of the performer and the immaterial body of the projection in *Snows*, or in the destructive splitting of the filmstrip, and the splintering of Nicolson's on-screen image under her needle in *Reel Time*, both artists reconfigure cinema as an active and discursive space of dialogue and enquiry not only between viewer and screen, but between the different bodies instrumental in its operations, including that of the artist herself. In the intermingling of these bodies: corporeal, mechanical, material and immaterial, the experience of cinema is thus re-imagined as a tactile and reciprocal event, a series of simultaneous dialogues, or 'material equations', of which the viewer is both witness and participant.

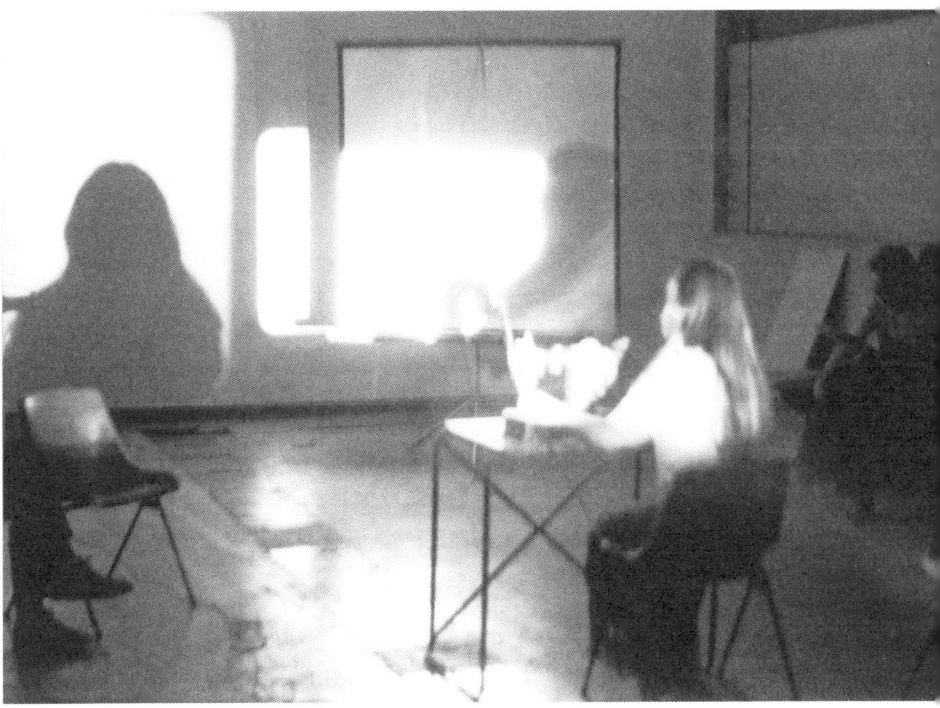

Annabel Nicolson, *Reel Time* (1973): documentation of performance and film event. Courtesy the artist.

ENDNOTES

(1) Carolee Schneeman, *More Than Meat Joy: Performances and Selected Writings* (New York: Documentext, McPherson and Company, 2000), p. 97.

(2) *Ibid.* p. 63.

(3) John Sayre, *The Object of Performance: The American Avant-Garde Since 1970* (University of Chicago Press, London, 1989), p. 14.

(4) Amelia Jones, *Body Art: Performing the Subject* (Minneapolis: University of Minnesota Press, 1998), p. 14.

(5) Jean Michel Baudry, Ideological Effects of the Basic Apparatus, reprinted in, ed. Philip Rosen, *Narrative, Apparatus, Ideology* (Columbia University Press, New York, 1986), p. 294.

(6) Carolee Schneeman, *More Than Meat Joy: Performances and Selected Writings*, p. 129.

(7) Carolee Schneeman, 'Expanded Cinema: Free Form Recollection of New York', written to David Curtis on the occasion of the Underground Film Festival at the National Film Theatre, September 1970. Reprinted in ed. Duncan White, *Expanded Cinema: Art, Performance, Film* (Tate, London 2011), p. 96.

(8) As Schneeman explained: 'All performance elements: film, slides, lights, tapes, sequences, durations, sculptural light machine, determined by audience response. Contact mikes under their seats relay their motions and sounds; SCR switching systems feed into color organ, amplification from which we (performers) took cues.'
Carolee Schneeman, 'Expanded Cinema: Free Form Recollection of New York', p. 96.

(9) Carolee Schneeman, *More Than Meat Joy: Performances and Selected Writings*, p. 129.

(10) For a good account of Riegl and his development of theories of the haptic see Antonia Lant, 'Haptical Cinema,' *October*, issue 104, vol 74, Autumn 1995, pp. 45-73.

(11) Laura U Marks, *The Skin of the Film: Intercultural Cinema, Embodiment and the Senses* (Durham, London: Duke University Press, 2000), p. 162.

(12) *Ibid.* p. 163.

(13) David Levi Strauss, 'Love Rides Aristotle Through the Audience: Body, Image, and Idea in the Work of Carolee Schneeman,' *Carolee Schneeman, Up to and Including Her Limits* (New York: New Museum of Contemporary Art), p. 27.

(14) Malcolm le Grice, 'Real TIME/SPACE,' *Art and Artists*, Dec 1972, p. 39.

(15) Malcolm le Grice, *Abstract Film and Beyond* (Massachusetts, London: MIT Press, 1977), p. 148.

(16) See Lucy Reynolds, 'Reinterpreting Reel Time', *Film Waves*, Issue 24, Spring 2004, pp. 10-13.

(17) It is only in recent years that other, more subjective, feminist readings have been made of the gendered play between the apparatus of the sewing machine and the film projector in *Reel Time*. See: Felicity Sparrow, Annabel Nicolson: The Art of Light and Shadow, Artist's Profile, Luxonline, www.luxonline.org.uk/artists/annabel_nicolson/essay(2).html and Lucy Reynolds, 'Reinterpreting Reel Time', *Film Waves*, Issue 24, Spring 2004.

(18) Annabel Nicolson in conversation with Lucy Reynolds, January 2004.

(19) For an expansion of the use of shadow play in British expanded cinema see: Lucy Reynolds, 'Magic Tricks? The use of the shadow in British Expanded Cinema,' *Afterall*, Issue 23, Spring 2010.

(20) Walter Benjamin, 'Some Motifs in Baudelaire', *Illuminations* (New York: Schocken, 1969), p. 188.

(21) Laura Marks, *The Skin of the Film: Intercultural Cinema, Embodiment, and the Senses*, p. 191.

The Gesture of the Muted Voice: Cara Tolmie's *Myriad Mouth Line*

ISLA LEAVER-YAP

At first glance, Cara Tolmie's *Myriad Mouth Line* (2011) presents us with three gestures: of a body, a voice, and an explanation.[1] The performance begins with Tolmie slowly walking around the edges of a minimal stage area, which contains a microphone stand replete with mic, swivel chair, and amplifier unit (frame one). As she traces the perimeter, Tolmie sings two alternating notes before walking up to the microphone and singing a wordless melody (frame two). Then, posturing with arms raised and outstretched towards the audience, her body presents an emphatic gesture whose stress remains nonetheless recondite given the lack of verbal content. Holding this pose, Tolmie retreats to the centre of the stage to sit on the chair. She pivots on the seat, moving in a circle, her static bodily gesture transformed into rotating display. Tolmie then begins to describe a mythopoetic scenario where the narrator is: 'petrified into a clumsy mass and mocked by the oscillating perimeters now encircling me.' Closing her dense recitation, she adds: 'And another thing: "jurisdiction" – it's not a word digestible by the mouths of the myriad line' (frame three). Tolmie gets up from the chair and walks around the edge of the stage again, this time with microphone in hand, and emits an alarming series of shrill screeches, clicks and beats. Moving erratically around the stage she comes full circle to return to the chair (frame four). Once seated, she picks up a piece of paper and recites a text listing all the actions of her performance in chronological order. The text contains a seemingly objective analysis of each frame, its duration, content, rationale and frame number. She concludes definitively: 'We have now reached the end of the performance' (frame five).

Body. Voice. Explanation. There is a slippery movement here. Tolmie's body and voice appear largely in the abstract throughout this performance, and their coherence relies on the narrative of the closing explanation in frame five. Significantly, too, this is a voice that doesn't always speak, although it does attempt to 'interpret' at the end. The language and tone of the explanation is self-reflexive and impersonal. Yet it is significant that this is a performance of an explanation; its authenticity is deferred, bracketed as it is *within* the performance proper. The schism presented, then, is between the immaterial properties of performance: the voice and the word, the abstract gesture and its relation to the making of meaning.

In his highly influential lecture series, *How to Do Things with Words*, JL Austin states: 'to say something is to do something; or in which by saying or in saying something we are doing something.'(2) Remarkably, Austin never concerned himself much with the role of the voice within his analysis of the speech act.(3) Yet one wonders – when the voice bypasses the moment of saying something and skips directly to the 'doing', a different system of signification must surely arise. The mute voice might not say anything but it can still sound, still gesture. What, then, is the gesture of the muted voice? Anne Carson observes the wordlessness of Lazarus, the man who had to die twice: 'Even in the painting of [his resurrection] by Giotto, notice the person with raised hands and no mouth (perhaps his sister) placed behind Lazarus to load this space with muteness'.(4) Lazarus may be mute but his wordlessness is not without a sublime and transgressive function – a movement that passes in and out of language. Even without words, the body and the voice can create their own conditions, its own space and structure. Even without words, emotional conditioning can be brought into play. Let us concentrate here on that which emerges from the gesturing body: the voice.

The voice that does but does not speak has historically been a quandary for some philosophers and a blind spot for others. Sophokles, for example, speaks fearfully of the Athenian nymph Echo, a girl with 'no door on her mouth' – surely a terrifying thought for a man who describes silence as 'the good order' for women.(5) For Louis Althusser, the voice that speaks is akin to a Pygmalion event, a power that calls a subject into being through the voice's incantation. (6) Yet Althusser dedicates his argument only to the speaking voice, not the wordless one. Theodor Adorno, meanwhile, claims to separate music and language. But no sooner than stating, 'The person who takes music literally as language will be led astray by it,' he goes on to suggest: 'Questions, exclamations, subordinate clauses are everywhere, voices rise and fall, and, in all of this, the gesture of music is borrowed from the speaking voice.' Perhaps the problem of address lies in the hegemony of the written word and the proclivity to apply linguistic methodology to non-linguistic forms. Carolyn Abbate laments that such a common move transforms music and its attendant properties into 'a ventriloquist's dummy,' made to service any interpretation.(7) What is clear from these philosophical pronouncements, however, is that the musical voice, or rather the voice that appears with melody and without words, possesses an uncertain agency – free, or so it seems, from reference.

Comprising sound, image and text, often situated within performative scenarios, Tolmie's practice probes the conditions through which meaning is made, as well as the space that such meanings might require for intelligibility. If a recurring component can be gleaned from Tolmie's performance style, one might finds its closest parallel in the function of the Greek *khoros* (chorus) in classical theatre. *Khoros* serves both as a description of a song accompanied by dance, as well as the name for the figure or group that performs the song (and when in a group, the *khoros* often speaks simultaneously or in echo with one another). The presence of the *khoros* delineates the duration of action, with its members entering and exiting to mark the start and end of the play, while its narrative function acts to make sense of the actions on the stage and to reflect on what has come before. The comparison here is informative; firstly, because the performance structure of the *khoros* – the interrelationship of movement, duration and sound – is a repeating form in Tolmie's performances; and secondly, because the making of meaning is the primary function both of the *khoros* and the central concern of Tolmie's practice.

For an event at the Chisenhale Gallery, London, Tolmie presented *She do the policeman in different voices* (2010), a performance that begins with the recitation of a text that variously ruminates on dog shit, communality and memory.(8) Riffing on the format of an artist's lecture, Tolmie finished her reading with a quote from Karl Marx – 'one must force the frozen circumstances to dance by singing to them their own melody' – before launching into a loud karaoke rendition of the faux-folk song 'Caledonia'; this is a song that, one might say, says nothing but its sound is affective nonetheless.

The desire to rupture the convention of the art performance in order to manipulate the tensions that arise from both performing and viewing such events, and to find a way to break with sincerity through comic or even inappropriate behaviour is key to Tolmie's intentions. As the artist notes with a certain wryness:

> *Everyone likes to be sung to, and maybe you can play with those desires. The emotional dynamic of performance and the feeling of tension within that space can be subjected to a*

> *kind of dispersal, like a discharging of emotional tension that somehow also has the potential to shine a criticality on whatever has come before it. I felt this way about the use of 'Sinner Man' by Nina Simone at the end of* Inland Empire *(David Lynch, 2006)* (9)

The insertion of an incongruous emotional component into the performance points not only to the salient limits of audience expectation, but also to the conditions through which meaning is made, as well as how meaning is (or is not) permitted. In other words, the acceptable flow of performance is unacceptable to Tolmie, who instead uses interruption to attenuate points of discomfort and unfamiliarity. In the manner of cinema, her performances splice in external or unlikely elements that works through affect rather than through reason. In the case of *She do the policeman...*, for example, Tolmie sings a manufactured saccharine ballad (which has an awkward relationship to the artist's national identity), while in another performance, *The Interview*, she sings Connie Francis' 'Who's Sorry Now' to conclude a performance lecture. In both instances, Tolmie probes the conditions of performance, noting, 'We've invented structural rules in order to understand phenomena that connects us to the sentimental side of our human existences. However, in doing this we have also created a force which can obliterate the legitimacy of that human experience, making us feel ashamed of our naiveté.' (10) Tolmie's practice seeks to challenge the claustrophobia of these validating forms and, working within the format of art-performance, she develops her own structure of movement, voice and unlikely anthems that collide to create an encounter that might reconcile affect with experience that is, significantly, without immediate recourse to external forms of legitimation.

fig. 18 — *Myriad Mouth Line* dramatically extends Tolmie's attempt to constitute a temporary space of affect so clearly evidenced in previous works such as *She do the policeman...*, *The Interview*, and *Room Studies* (2010). (11) But, unlike the aforementioned performances, the dominant form of *Myriad Mouth Line* is the unspeaking voice that reverberates with a structural strangeness, unmoored from recognisable narrative and logical causality. Using the voice to demarcate a space (less a site of performance than of possibility), Tolmie's temporary vocal architecture refuses the forms of appropriation common to her previous works; her actions rarely refer to anything that lies beyond this vocal perimeter. (12) Through their insistent repetition, the two notes sung at the beginning of the performance serve as the base notes from which to extrude a melody, while the ensuing inchoate actions (both gestural and aural) that make up the performance as a whole are the reference points for the concluding analysis. Thus *Myriad Mouth Line* not only creates an autonomous landscape made up of its internal and largely undisclosed logic but also exhaustively bulwarks this self-sufficiency through the reuse of its temporary materials and ensuing auto-critique. Essentially comprising a series of irrational actions extrapolated into the appearance of a logical sequence, *Myriad Mouth Line* declares its own legitimacy without the need to resort to external forms of knowledge and without the primacy of the word.

*

To maintain meaning and communicative power, words are never unique instances but contain within every utterance a phantom history of their previous use, context and life. The pre-habitation of language drags up old voices with each articulation. This is the inevitable dialogical nature of our present that is always in reflection with the past – a 'double-voiced discourse', as Bakhtin would have it.(13) But what speaks when the voice speaks? Blanchot attempts to answer this question with a paradox that articulates less the content of the speaking than its architecture: 'It manifests itself in a space of redoubling, of echo and resonance where it is not someone, but rather this unknown space - its discordant accord, its vibration - that speaks without speaking.'(14) The voice that does without words stands within a vacuum; it must generate its own associations and emotions according to its own logic. *Myriad Mouth Line* asks a similar question. In her excavation of the wordless gesture both through the body and the voice, Tolmie seeks not to simply lay the structures of performance bare but to also develop an emotional register that might counter the authority of language that seeks to regulate those emotions...

jurisdiction – it's not a word digestible by the mouths of the myriad line.

ENDNOTES

(1) Cara Tolmie, *Myriad Mouth Line* (2011): performance occurring daily 12-15 October 2011 outside the Frieze Art Fair, Regent's Park, London. http://vimeo.com/35678720 Last accessed 15 March 2012. The 'frames' referred to in this text are taken from Tolmie's *Myriad Mouth Line*.

(2) JL Austin, *How to Do Things with Words*, eds. J. O. Urmson and Marina Sbish (Cambridge Massachusetts: Harvard University Press, 1962), p. 12.

(3) For further discussion relating Austin's writings to speech and the performative utterance see Michelle Duncan, 'The operatic scandal of the singing body', *Cambridge Opera Journal*, Vol. 16, No. 3, Nov. 2004, p. 289.

(4) Anne Carson, *Nox* (New York: New Directions, 2010), section 8.4.

(5) Taken from Anne Carson's translations of Sophokles in Carson, 'The Gender of Sound', in *Glass, Irony and God* (New York: New Directions, 1995), p. 119-139. All spellings follow the Greek as used by Carson.

(6) Louis Althusser, 'Ideology and Ideological State Apparatuses', in *Lenin and Philosophy and Other Essays*, trans. Ben Brewster (New York: Monthly Review Press, 1971), p. 177.

(7) Carolyn Abbate, *Unsung voices: opera and musical narrative in the nineteenth century* (New Jersey: Princeton University Press, 1996), p. 18.

(8) Cara Tolmie, *She do the policeman in different voices* (2010): performance as part of Manuela Gernedel and Morag Keil's event for *21st Century*, Chisenhale Gallery, London, 26 January 2010. Tolmie's title is taken from a phrase TS Eliot initially considered using for *The Wasteland*, 'He do the Policeman in Different Voices', which appears in Charles Dickens' *Our Mutual Friend* (1865).

(9) Cara Tolmie in conversation with author, 10 March 2012.

(10) This is and is not Tolmie speaking. In fact, this is Tolmie restaging words she spoke in a question-and-answer interview with friend and writer John Douglas Miller. Tolmie recited the conversation, speaking both parts, as part of *The Interview* (2008), a performance that concluded with Tolmie's rendition of 'Who's Sorry Now?', the song popularised by Connie Francis in 1958. Cara Tolmie, *The Interview*, 20 December 2008, performance, *Event Horizon*, GSK Contemporary, Royal Academy of Arts, London.

(11) Cara Tolmie, *Room Studies* (2010): performance, Tramway, Glasgow, 26 June 2010.

(12) While Bruce Nauman's minimally performative *Walking in an exaggerated manner* (1967-68) and Meredith Monk's episodic, gestural abstractions in *16mm Earrings* (1966/77) might serve as formal insights into the actions of *Myriad Mouth Line*, the primacy of Tolmie's vocal action is more usefully regarded as internally referential. In terms of the artist's own references, Tolmie notes *Myriad Mouth Line* emerged as an extension of *The end is a tumultuous noise* (2010), a performance and text work Tolmie performed as part of *The Voice is a Language* programme, Tramway, Glasgow and curated by the author. The full text from Tolmie's *The end is a tumultuous noise* can be found at voiceisalanguage.wordpress.com (last accessed 16 March 2012).

(13) Mikhail Bakhtin, 'Discourse in Dostoyevsky', in *Problems of Dostoevsky's Poetics*, trans. Caryl Emerson (Minneapolis: University of Minnesota Press, 1984), p. 185.

(14) Maurice Blanchot, '10. "The voice, not speech", Atheism and Writing, Humanism and the Cry', in *The Infinite Conversation*, trans. Susan Hanson (Minneapolis: University of Minnesota, 1993), p. 258.

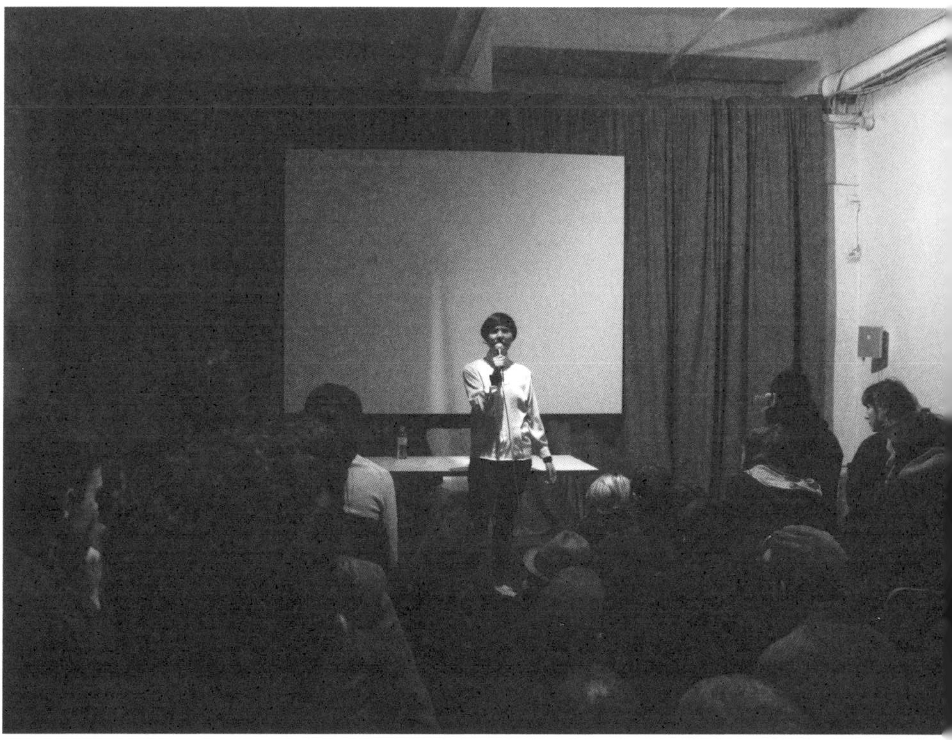

Cara Tolmie, *She do the policeman in different voices* 2010: performance documentation.

The Divided Stage: Splitting the Dialectics of Performance

PIL AND GALIA KOLLECTIV

Walter Benjamin described Bertolt Brecht's 'epic theatre' as a form that wishes to fill in the orchestra pit, standing for the 'abyss which separates the players from the audience as it does the dead from the living'.(1) The specialised organisation, architecture and tradition of the theatre, according to Benjamin, elevate the stage far above the audience, in a literal sense, but also above its mythical origins rooted in ritual where the aesthetic language of drama was not yet distinguishable from the social fabric of life itself. This idea of the distancing of the mediated aesthetic space from a lived reality, rehearsed again and again throughout the last century in the writing of many influential authors from Guy Debord to Nicolas Bourriaud, addresses the space of cultural production as a duality. Thus, paradoxically, to reproduce life convincingly on the stage, the 19th century theatre that preceded Brecht had to deploy specialist and artificial means and so, paradoxically, remove itself completely from the real conditions of life outside the theatre. In other words, the problem that Benjamin identifies through Brecht is one of a dialectic in which the two worlds – the one existing on stage and the other in the seats of the audience – define each other through a mutuality from which they are unable to set themselves free.

The typical solution to this problem offered by the modernist dramaturge is to invert these dialectical relations. Brecht, says Benjamin, transforms the action that belongs to the audience – observing, interpreting, thinking – into the chief action portrayed on the stage. The character of the thinker, rather than that of the doer, becomes in his work the main protagonist, while the development of the story is interspersed with moments of pause, in which the audience is asked directly to translate this thinking or observing into a political or ethical act of judgment. The theatrical spectacle makes its artificial nature known, resulting in the rupture of the cathartic identification of the audience with the characters on stage.

Through this alienation or estrangement, the replacement of catharsis with the process of questioning, the entire world outside the theatre becomes de-natured and shows itself to be also an artificial environment, authored and managed by particular forces. Conversely, in Antonin Artaud's Theatre of Cruelty, the opposition is collapsed. And yet, as noted by Jacques Rancière, this project of minimising the distance between life and theatre effects a similar disavowal of representation.(2)

However, following the gradual transition in the west over the last fifty years from industrial to post industrial economies, this set of questions and artistic strategies has lost some of its *raison d'être*. Although much of the critical discourse surrounding art still relies on outdated dialectical and anti-representational notions similar to Brecht's, the relationship between theatre and its double has been significantly altered in this time. Many artists and theoreticians are still engaged in a project of collapsing the boundaries between the actual and the representational by challenging the dichotomies of author/audience, gallery/community, commodity/experience and so on. But, as the writers associated with the Italian post-autonomist movement have noted, the organisation of work and of the structures of capitalist exploitation of labour power are increasingly based on the theatrical techniques of the avant-garde. As part of the landscape of work today, characters, narratives, experiences and theatrical settings are produced, managed and analysed, producing value directly from the social reality of human relations.

Work is no longer the silent space of Fordism from which communication, debate, analysis and play are excluded. On the contrary, telling stories, assuming characters and constructing social situations are all procedures that are required in order to be a successful post-Fordist worker. To illustrate, this we can look at a moment that became almost a post-modern cinematic cliché: to supplement her income, the busy suburban mother starts working in the phone sex industry. She answers the phone to speak to one of her regular clients and assumes the character of a latex clad dominatrix while changing a diaper with her other hand and while she also does not neglect to check up on the dinner warming in the oven. Beyond the obvious ironic gap between fantasy and reality, and beyond the loss of directness and the greater degree of technological mediation through which human relations are filtered, this scenario reveals something about the nature of post-Fordist labour. This is of course an unusual case (although by most estimates the phone sex industry generates billions of dollars in profit every year in the US alone) but in its assimilation of theatrical techniques it is not unlike many other, more mainstream occupations. The phone sex worker's product is the character that she or he constructs, and the main tools of this job are communicative and affective. The work is fragmented, full of interruptions and conflicting demands: it invades the domestic space via the telephone line and in return is interrupted by the demands of the everyday. The characters are produced without any real conviction or believability: they are selected from a large catalogue of possible personalities and delivered by the worker without real investment in the natural or mimetic quality of the work. It is easy to see in this case why the Brechtian techniques of alienation – the breaks in the story, revealing the equipment supporting the play, presentation of the psychology and actions of characters as inconsistent – lose their critical value. Rather than producing a critical distance and fermenting a revolutionary sentiment, these techniques are subsumed into capitalist production and work only to enhance existing structures of oppression and inequality.

Many writers have asserted that there is no outside to capitalism, or 'no alternative', to use Margaret Thatcher's words. It is in response to this impasse that Alain Badiou turns to the inverted dialectics of Mao Zedong as a way forward. If Capitalism presents us with a totality, then political action is to be found in a forced division of a totality into two positions. This operation, writes Badiou, is inherently anti-dialectical (at least in the Hegelian sense), since it does not put forward a synthesis of two antithetical positions in which the opposition nostalgically yearns to be unified with the 'One' from which it was born. A division of 'One into Two' produces renewal without a teleological unification of oppositions into a totality. The split does not produce a resolution: instead, the 'question of the new immediately becomes the question of the creative division in the singularity of the situation'.**(3)** Badiou borrows this inversion of dialectics from Maoist thinking and in particular from Mao Zedong's 'Examples of Dialectics' from 1959. Against the background of the failure of the 'great leap forward' and a growing rift in the communist world between China and Russia, Mao claimed that communist thinking in China must resist the notion of a stable plateau of socialism and encourage new contradictions to emerge from the seeming unity. He even finds the possibility of an ideological opposite to socialism coming out of the party itself as a sign of good health:

> *Let them go in for capitalism …If one only goes in for socialism and not for capitalism, isn't that too simple? Wouldn't we then lack the unity of opposites, and be merely one-sided? Let them*

> *do it. Let them attack us madly, demonstrate in the streets, take up arms to rebel — I approve all of these things. Society is very complex, there is not a single commune, a single hsien, a single department of the Central Committee, in which one cannot divide into two.*(4)

Badiou identifies Maoist dialectics as a form of thinking politics that does not allow ideological closures such as the free market socialism that exists in China today. In an unattributed short essay from 1992, 'The Dialectical Mode: With Regard to Mao Zedong and Problems of Strategy in China's Revolutionary War', he describes this methodology as a dialectics different from: 'the image of the "turn about" or flip-flop'.(5) In contradiction to Hegelian dialectics, the Maoist version does not assume an empty place or outside of the current conditions within which it can grow and evolve as an antithetical position. The Maoist split from within, says Badiou, does not look for closures or stability of theory and therefore is particularly adequate for the philosophical task of thinking through change itself: '...if we consider an entity in its becoming, in the way it transforms itself, its name will be a contradictory multiplicity. The [Maoist] dialectical mode has at its center a dialectical materialism of transformation'.(6) Leaving to one side Badiou's actual defence of the cultural revolution as a historical event, we would like to apply the model with which he presents us to the dialectic of the theatre that we have been examining.

Perhaps the best example of this practice of splitting of a totality presented in a theatrical context is the play within Brian De Palma's film *Hi Mom!* (1970), starring Robert De Niro. In the film, De Niro's character becomes involved with a black activist theatre group. For their performance, 'Be Black, Baby', the group invite an audience of white middle class theatre-goers to partake in 'the black experience'. Initially, this seems like a typical participatory performance project, albeit a rather uncomfortable prospect for the participants. They are asked to touch the performers' hair, loosen their hips and eat soul food. When they complain that they are merely the audience and do not wish to participate, it is explained to them that they too are actors now. Their attempts to squeamishly reject a taste of pig feet are met with forceful insistence. Things quickly degenerate to the point where the white audience, by now in black-face, are assaulted by the black actors whose faces are now covered in white makeup, with one woman nearly raped. In the nick of time, a white policeman shows up – played by De Niro. But of course he is in on the act, and turns out to defend the (whited-up) black actors and further assault and abuse the white 'audience'. It is here that the liberal, white audience's views are put to the test. The film cynically shows them leaving the venue, shaken but also exhilarated at having truly had the 'black experience'. But the play is not about verisimilitude. It doesn't just convey an experience through audience participation, but rather, it identifies the fissures within the progressive mindset that allow racism to persist insidiously in a society that preaches tolerance.

'Be Black, Baby' offers a different model of criticality for the theatre because it circumvents the obvious pitfalls of the modernist dialectical model. In this context, it is important to mention that the play dealt with here is part of a film and is, therefore, only ever presented through the mediation of cinema. The idea that the theatre can offer an authentic experience of blackness is even more absurd since it is doubly removed, through cinematic framing, from 'life'. In the long scenes devoted to the play in *Hi Mom!*, the camera assumes a very active role, buzzing around the actors and the audience as if it too were a character. In some shots, the action of the actors is obscured from view, while others are too dark for the viewer to see clearly, mimicking the style of *cinéma vérité*. Stylised filmic interventions are also used in a deliberately noticeable manner. De Palma uses sharp cuts and dynamic angles and, more importantly, direct documentary-style interviews with members of the audience. The relationship between theatre and cinema is of course not coincidental in *Hi Mom!*.

Benjamin describes Brecht's epic theatre as similar to film, full of cuts, gaps and transitions from one scene to the next. These gaps are there, as mentioned earlier, for the audience to reflect on what it is being shown but also for the actor who also can find a distance from the character portrayed. '[A]n actor', writes Benjamin: 'should reserve for himself the possibility of stepping out of character artistically... [and] insist on portraying a man who reflects about his part'.[7] Brecht sees the actor as caught in a dialectical relationship with the subject he or she portrays, a relationship in which each produces the other. Rather than the complete and neutral convergence of the character and the actor, the Brechtian actor sets two types of performances one against the other, one of action and one of contemplation. But, Benjamin adds, this is not akin to the liberal play of possible identities that is the transgression permitted by the system. Brecht's actors are not asked to identify with a different position in a way that is tolerable and inoffensive like (Benjamin's example) a devout husband and father portraying Don Juan. Here, the actions of the characters on stage contradict completely the ethical judgment of the actors: a German actor in exile who is asked to assume the character of a murderous Nazi SS officer, for example.

Da Palma teases out of this relationship between theatre and cinema an even more direct political significance. The main protagonist of the film, Vietnam veteran John Rubin (the police man who arrives to intervene in the chaos ensuing from the play, 'Be Black, Baby'), seeks to establish his relationship to his surroundings through the mediation of the lens. While he takes an almost passive role in his own life, the camera dictates all his artistic, economic, sexual and social engagements with the city he returns to from the first truly 'live' (...on you television screen) war in history. In the first part of the film, for example, Rubin is attempting to create a new brand of pornography (or art) by spying on and filming the intimate lives of his neighbours. But *Hi Mom!* is not another Hollywood film moralising against the corrupting power of the media. Rubin's passivity introduces a new type of political subject: a person, or even simply a body, who records the actions of others via technology and is captured by others in a similar way. He is a post-Foucauldian panoptic subject who captures other subjects with his gaze at the same time that these technologies of ordering through observation operate on him. Thus, the character's agency is not derived here from a liberal difference, from actions or ideas that are set apart and against other ones. Instead, agency is achieved through mimesis: copying and reproducing the world, reordering it through looking.

Similarly, the performers of 'Be Black, Baby' don't inhabit characters but rather mimic stereotypes. The effect of their performance does not rely on the liveness of the experience. It is enough for their audience to serve as proxies for us because we don't need to be convinced by this performance. Instead the film asks us to question any performance of authenticity. At the same time, it is literally impossible to separate the performers from their acting: are the actors antagonistic towards the audience because they are black militants encountering members of the hegemony or are they simply enacting the role of the aggressors outside the theatre (such as, the police, cultural and educational institutions)? 'Be Black, Baby' does not allow for ethical stability and the positions articulated by the actors cannot be open to debate and deliberation. Benjamin argues that identification with your tormentor is impossible, but the actors here are shown enjoying the subversive assuming of the role of hegemony and we are left incapable of the ethical judgment asked for by Brecht: can we approve of the sexual assault of audience members in the name of artistic freedom? If members of the audience are told that they are actors too now, do they stop performing once they leave the theatre?

'Be Black, Baby' may have been intended as a satire, but it leaves the viewer with a lot of uncomfortable questions. The audience of the play might learn little from the experience, but for us, the audience of the film, there is nowhere to hide: we see ourselves reflected in their smug admiration for the experience they've just had and that response is foreclosed for us. The avoidance of an ethical ground forces a new split into the political map whose existing oppositions are complicit with racial inequality. The racist position, that there is an essential biological difference between races, is obviously questioned here. The performative reversal of behaviours (when black actors in white faces become racist aggressors) clearly demonstrates how cultural and political differences are produces as exactly that – non-essentialist social behavior. But, the other position of mainstream American society in the late 1960s, that of the liberal audience who, from a position of sympathy, wishes to adopt the otherness of black culture as 'cool', is also challenged and exposed as racist. If the play in De Palma's film is an illustration that the otherness of African Americans is produced as a direct result of the power structures in which they operate and if the behaviour of the audience confirms this, then both the positive-liberal and negative-racist understandings of this otherness are exposed as political fantasies that ultimately support inequality. When the liberal and the racist are grouped together a new political fissure opens up, this time not between the admirers and debasers of black culture but between an understanding of race as an inherent quality of the individual and the understanding of race as a performance built on socio-political signifiers.

The type of encounter theatre depicted by De Palma stems from the same tradition that Rancière blames for the survival of the Platonic suspicion towards representation. As such De Palma's theatrical model presented in 'Be Black, Baby' pairs the immersive theatre of cruelty with anti-theatrical Brechtian techniques, at once producing a realism that transgresses the boundaries of art and life and imposing a critical distance and awareness of artifice on participants. But instead of reasserting the dialectic of the theatre and lived reality, De Palma's theatre attacks the assumptions underlying both the audience's engagement with this representation of race relations and the tenability of their politics outside the context of the theatre. 'Be Black, Baby' quickly dismisses the theatrical engagement with the gap between the everyday and representation. Because what is represented on stage here in 'documentary' style is in fact the stereotype of an ethnic group and because it is performed by the audience rather then the actors, there is never any expectation of authenticity or suspension of disbelief. The white middle class audience knows full well that the suggestion that it can somehow be magically transformed into poor black people simply by applying paint to their faces is absurd – almost as ridiculous as the liberal idea that skin colour does not matter in the American society of the late 60s. Instead of this engagement with authenticity and artifice, the play forces us to locate the tension elsewhere, not in the relationship of the stage and its double but between the different types of performances that are fighting over the theatricality of public space or the performativity of everyday life.

We can see a similar logic at work in the performances of fig. 19 the Israeli art group, Public Movement, whose motto states: 'the army did not demonstrate sufficient creativity'. Appearing in dress uniform, they mimic state rallies and folk dancing, holding hands in a circle, crossing their feet, rearranging themselves into a marching phalanx, giving speeches and singing in city squares. These acts are often juxtaposed with car crashes, riots and terrorist attacks, presented in an equally dispassionate, stylised fashion. Here, again, the point is not to establish a critical distance from the action, which is presented as a kind of ritual and really does function in the same way as an official ceremony. We are not invited to view the appropriation of militaristic choreography as ironic, nor are we ever comfortable in succumbing to its seduction. But by juxtaposing Zionist state aesthetics with collective trauma, Public Movement reveals both to be equally ritualised in the responses they elicit. The unity of the performances that govern our movements in public and the private emotions we associate with them is split from within to the point where we can no longer be certain of the boundaries between self determination and social construction. The stage is not shown to be any more or less artificial than the social constructs being portrayed and no gap opens between performers and their actions: in fact, Public Movement have been accused of being 'IDF propaganda minions'.(8) Yet the kind of propaganda they seem to manifest is also curiously dated, at odds both with the violent content of their work and with the post-ideological façade of the state in the name of fig. 20 which they purport to speak. Much like the band Crime, whose 1979 performance at the San Quentin prison saw them wearing uniforms identical to those worn by the guards policing their audience, Public Movement send mixed signals that lay bare tensions pre-existing in the unacknowledged performances they re-enact.

If the move we describe here rejects the established dialectical procedures of the avant garde that have lost their criticality, it is vital to think specifically how this proposal could rejuvenate the potential of theatre against the developments in post-Fordist labour mentioned above. The alienated distance that Brecht wanted to create for his audiences in order to invite a deconstruction of political structures is the prevailing mode of late capitalist production. A distance, even cynicism, is assumed as a given in this system: in its purest form, the self-motivated, self-managed 'portfolio career' of the creative industries, the post-Fordist labourer exploits him- or herself. One is literally one's own boss and, at the same time, still a worker. The power that operates on the worker is assimilated into the psyche and as such disappears from view. The image of the factory, the power station or the slum, which served as concrete illustrations of the battleground between different classes in the first half of the 20th century, have also disappeared from this landscape to be replaced by the translucence of digital technology. This is disappearance is conveyed in countless science fiction films: in *Minority Report*, for example, the panoptic machine of the police is a transparent board of liquid and malleable digital information.

If the architecture of power melts away in the new creative cities of post-Fordism, theatre can make it concrete again by making present the explicit ideology that is treated as abject by late capitalism. We might not be able to escape dialectical critique altogether but the dialectic we are proposing here does not require an inherently weak position external to power with which to address power. We do not need to expose the corruption or immorality of power, facts of which we are all cynically aware and which change nothing. An exaggeration of the performance of the already highly theatricalised rites and rituals that we inhabit daily is able to concretise the postulations of life-style gurus, managerial help books and psych-lite literature as ideological manifestos, embodying the contradictions that sustain them beyond the point of sustainability and splitting the totality of this world in two.

ENDNOTES

(1) Walter Benjamin, 'What is Epic Theatre', *Illuminations* (London: Fontana, 1992), p. 150.

(2) Jacques Ranciere, 'The Emancipated Spectator', *Artforum*, March, 2007.

(3) Alain Badiou, 'One Divides itself into Two', in: *Lenin Reloaded: Toward a Politics of Truth*, eds. Sebastian Budgen, Eustache Kouvélakis and Slavoj Žižek (Durham, NC: Duke University Press, 2007), p. 11.

(4) Mao Zedong, 'Talk On Questions Of Philosophy, August 18, 1964', available at: www.marxists.org/reference/archive/mao/selected-works/volume-9/mswv9_27.htm Last accessed 23.05.2011.

(5) Anonymous, 'The Dialectical Mode: With Regard to Mao Zedong and Problems of Strategy in China's Revolutionary War', in: *Positions*, Bruno Bosteels - tr., Duke University Press, 13:3, Winter, 2005, p. 666-7. Originally in *La Distance Politique*, issue 3, May, 1992. Despite texts appearing anonymously in this publication, the essay has been widely ascribed to Badiou.

(6) *Ibid.* p. 667.

(7) Walter Benjamin, 'What is Epic Theatre', p.150.

(8) Daniel Miller, 'Performing Politics for Germany', *Frieze*, 13.7.2009, available at: blog.frieze.com/performing_politics_for_germany/ Last accessed 27.3.12.

ALAIN BADIOU teaches a popular seminar at the Collège International de Philosophie, on topics ranging from the great 'antiphilosophers' (Saint-Paul, Nietzsche, Wittgenstein, Lacan) to the major conceptual innovations of the 20th century. He is (with Sylvain Lazarus and Natacha Michel) at the centre of L'Organisation Politique, a post-party organization concerned with direct popular intervention in a wide range of issues (including immigration, labor, and housing). He is the author of several successful novels and plays as well as more than a dozen philosophical works.

BRIDGET CRONE is a curator and writer based in London working across the UK and internationally. Bridget was the director of Media Art Bath (2006-11) – a publicly funded commissioning organisation. She has a particular interest in contemporary moving image and performance practices. She has curated exhibitions and projects by artists including, Gail Pickering, Tom Nicholson, Clare Gasson, Pil and Galia Kollectiv; for organisations such as: Ian Potter Museum, Melbourne; Holburne Museum, Bath; and Arnolfini, Bristol and The Showroom, London.

VANESSA DESCLAUX is an independent curator and writer based in Paris. She is a practice-based researcher on the MPhil/PhD programme in Art at Goldsmiths College, London. Recent projects and exhibitions include her research on Matt Mullican as part of *Performance in Residence* with If I Can't Dance, I Don't Want to be Part of Your Revolution, Amsterdam; and *Ahoy, an island!*, curated with Marie Canet at FRAC Aquitaine, Bordeaux and Fondation Ricard, Paris.

ANNE-SOPHIE DINANT is Associate Curator at the South London Gallery. She has curated exhibitions of work by Manon de Boer, Charles Atlas and Mika Tajima (co-curated with Andrew Bonacina), as well as performance and film projects by artists such as: Eleanor Antin, Michel Journiac, Gisèle Vienne/Dennis Cooper/Jonathan Capdevielle, Claire Fontaine and Jessica Warboys. Among other independent projects, she has curated programmes at the Curzon Soho and the BFI.

ELIE DURING is Associate Professor in Philosophy at University of Paris-Ouest Nanterre. A Bergson specialist, he has contributed to the critical edition published by the Presses Universitaires de France. His current research focuses on the implications of the space-time concept for metaphysics and aesthetics, in relation to the moving image. He is the author of several papers on Alain Badiou (see 'Art', in A. J. Bartlett & J. Clemens (eds.), *Alain Badiou: Key Concepts*, Chesholm, Acumen, 2010).

BEATRICE GIBSON is an artist and filmmaker based in London. Employing the score as a paradigm for their production, her films explore voice, speech, collective production and the problems of their representation. She is currently working on a new film, co-commissioned by The Showroom London, and CAC Bretigny. Gibson's films are distributed by LUX, London and Argos, Belgium.

PIL AND GALIA KOLLECTIV are London based artists, writers and curators working in collaboration. Their work addresses the legacy of modernism and the way avant-garde discourses operate in the context of a changing landscape of creative work and instrumentalised leisure. They are also the directors of artist-run project space xero, kline & coma and contributing editors at Art Papers. They work as lecturers in Fine Art at the University of Reading.

ISLA LEAVER-YAP writes about and organises projects with artists. She was an editor of MAP magazine for four years and is a contributor to periodicals including Afterall and Mousse. At the Institute of Contemporary Arts (ICA), London, she co-organised *Nought to Sixty*, and began the ongoing ICA series Artists Film Club. She recently organised the exhibition series *Short Stories* at Sculpture Center, New York. She lives in New York.

LISA PANTING is a gallerist, curator and writer. In 2005 she co-founded Hollybush Gardens, London with Malin Ståhl. Between 2009 and 2011, she was the director of Picture This, Bristol where she commissioned new work by Yael Davids, Hito Steyerl and Maryam Jafri. She has taught at Central Saint Martins, participating in Double Agents, a research group convened by Anne Tallentire and Graham Ellard.

DOMINIC PATERSON is a lecturer in History of Art at the University of Glasgow, and is a visiting member of staff at Glasgow School of Art. Amongst his recent publications are essays on the work of: Lucy Gunning, Christine Borland and Martin Soto Climent. He is currently undertaking a research residency at Glasgow Sculpture Studios.

LUCY REYNOLDS is a lecturer and curator in artists' moving image. Her area of research focuses on expanded cinema and British avant-garde film of the 1970s. She presents talks on artists' film and video, and teaches the history and theory of artists' moving image across the UK. Recent publishing includes 'Magic Tricks? Shadow Play in British Expanded Cinema', in *The Expanded Cinema: Art, Performance, Film* by Afterall/Tate publications.

IAN WHITE is an artist working mainly in performance. From 2001 to 11 he was Adjunct Film Curator for the Whitechapel Gallery, London. He is the co-editor of *Kinomuseum: Towards an artists' cinema* and co-authored *We Are Behind* with Emily Wardill. He is the facilitator of the LUX Associate Artists Programme, London and in 2011-12 a tutor of the performance programme *practice-theatre* at the Dutch Art Institute, Arnhem.